Nail it.

# Nail it.

Create and deliver presentations
that connect, compel, and convince.

**Debbie Roth Fay**

PRESENTATION SOLUTIONS

Library of Congress Control Number: 2014917979
Bespeak Presentation Solutions, LLC,
Fairfield, CT
ISBN-13: 978-0692287859
ISBN-10: 069228785X
LCCN: 2014917979

www.nailitpresentations.com

beheard@bespeakpresentations.com

Cover design by Tracey Cameron

Layout by Laurie Curtis

# Dedication

For my parents, Bette and Bob,
the inspiration for this book and my work.
For my sister and brother, Diane and David,
my lifelong cheerleaders.
For my children, Jackie, Mackenzie, and Charlie,
my dreams come true.
For my bonus sons, Jesse and Julian,
the best gifts I have ever been given.
And for my husband, Michael,
who makes all things possible.

# Acknowledgments

In 2006 I decided to start my own public speaking coaching business, a dream I'd held for the better part of a decade. Without knowing a soul in business (or how to start a business), I began getting out and meeting people, speaking anywhere anyone would have me, and learning as I went. I wouldn't have been able to find my way without my business coach and sister, Diane Helbig. I would never have come up with the name for my company without my childhood friend Lisa Awrey. I lucked out when I met Tracie Valentino, the creator of my logo and website. My brother, David, loaned me his gifted artist's eye, gently steering me in the right direction. I am grateful to Carol Mazzarella and the women of the Fairfield (Connecticut) County Network of Executive Women for giving me my first speaking opportunity. To the members of the Independent Business Network (IBN) of Southport, Connecticut, for embracing me, encouraging me, and teaching me more about business than I ever could have learned on my own.

To all my clients, who trust me with their messages, their challenges, and their aspirations, and most important, themselves, I say thank you. A special thanks to Rita Smircich, my very first client, and to Ed Laflamme, my first "big project" client (and one of the best people I will ever know). To Ed Lloyd (another one of the best people I will ever know), Annie Abram, Mark Berardi, Scott Briggs, Dominic Broom, Matt Bud, Jason Diamond, Dawn Fay, John Ferrer, Ron Garonzik, Micki Hoesly, Ed Kelly, Kathy Lamarr-Bines, Kathy McShane, Mike Meakem, Heidi Michaels, Dan Mullane, Damian Mullen, Jane Pollak, Shauna Reilly, Christine Rivers, Aaron Rulnick, Bill Sims, David Skoczen, Karen Spanard, Lisa St. Germain, Mary Beth Sullivan, Meiki Tollman,

Tulin Tuzel, and Daniel Verbruggen, thank you, thank you, thank you.

To everyone at Tauck in Norwalk, Connecticut, every one of whom makes me feel like family. (With a special thank you to Sharyn Cannon for bringing me in.)

To Jody Ferrer, my very first volunteer publicist; to Duane Cashin, Doug Ferguson, and Marc Tannenbaum, mentors and friends who gave me great advice and support. To my mastermind group: Olga Adler, Gillian Anderson, and Jessica Bram — you ladies are my team. To Nancy Simonds, my tireless book editor. To Lorraine Alexson, my copy editor, my superhero, who came to the rescue and saved this book. To Tracey Cameron, my brilliant, wildly talented cover designer. WOW. (And to my beloved Aunt Susan, who put the two of us together.) To Evan Skinner, my excellent, eternal, unofficial, and unpaid newsletter editor and my dear friend.

To my father, who sang and danced around the living room for me, instilling in me a love of the stage. To my original "coachees," my cousins, who suffered through my endless forced "rehearsals" and "performances" of *The Sound of Music*. To the Kinsleys, Marescas, and Petersons, who are cherished friends. And finally, to my mother and my aunts, five of the most accomplished, amazing women I know. You lit my way.

I thank you all.

# About the Author

**Debbie Roth Fay**

*Founder and President*
*Bespeak Presentation Solutions, LLC*

Debbie Roth Fay is the founder and president of Bespeak Presentation Solutions, LLC, providing presentation development, one-on-one public speaking coaching, and corporate training to businesses worldwide. An award-winning trainer and teacher with a lifelong involvement in theater, Debbie helps her clients present themselves with confidence, conviction, and clarity, delivering presentations that get heard and get results. Debbie is a sought-after speaker and contributing author to forbes.com and the Huffington Post.

For more information, go to:
www.bespeakpresentations.com

Facebook:
bespeak

Twitter:
@bespeak

# Contents

# Preface

Good news — there is nothing (or mostly nothing) in these pages that you don't already know in your gut. As you read, don't be surprised if you find yourself nodding your head and thinking, "I knew it." Because you did. You knew all along what makes a great presenter and a great presentation. How did you know? You've seen and heard good and bad presentations your whole life. Unfortunately, somewhere along the way some well-meaning teacher or professor or expert taught you or suggested to you some other method or process or trick, and despite the fact that in your gut it didn't feel right, you followed their lesson or advice and did it their way. Despite the fact that their way never felt right and never worked, you soldiered on, believing that they knew better than you. They didn't.

In this book are commonsense, easy-to-use, and impossible-to-forget tools for being a better presenter, building and delivering better and more effective presentations, starting now, today. There are no complicated acronyms, no crazy-making formulas, and most important, nothing that goes against your gut. The only thing required of you is to put these tools to work and use them every time you create and deliver a presentation. Use them and they will work. You will be a better, less nervous, more confident, compelling, change-making speaker.

In fact, not only will the ideas and tools outlined in this book make you a better, less nervous, more confident, compelling, change-making speaker, they'll make you a better, less nervous, more confident, compelling, change-making communicator. At the kitchen table, in the boardroom, at the PTA meeting, in the ballroom, or at the beach — wherever you are, and whomever you're with, you'll be just plain better. Better at convincing your kids to do their homework, better at getting your spouse to go see the movie you want to see, better at addressing a group of eight or eighty or telling a joke or a scary story. Better at being heard and getting results.

Read on. Time's a-wasting. And the world is in desperate need of what you have to say.

# Introduction

Whether you are speaking to one person or one thousand people, the goal of a presentation is for the presenter to get the message to the audience. Sounds pretty straightforward, right? But how many presentations have you walked out of having absolutely no earthly idea what the presenter's point was? Perhaps the speaker used terminology you were unfamiliar with, maybe an acronym or jargon word that left you with a big question mark in your head. Maybe he or she had PowerPoint slides that were so text-heavy you got dizzy and lost trying to read and then listen and then read and then . . . Or maybe there were really good points being made, just way too many of them for you to follow and remember. He or she may have been completely entertaining, engaging, hilarious even, and yet it's unclear what the whole thing was about.

This is a fate you do not want to befall you, the presenter. Your goal is to get your message across to your audience. Your goal is to inform, persuade, or both. Your goal is for the audience to understand your message, follow it all the way through, agree or adopt it, and remember it long after the presentation is over.

If you agree that the presenter, the message, and the audience are the three components of any presentation, let's look at each one and determine what role each plays, how each one affects the other, and what you need to know and do to ensure that your message, your presentation, is received, received well, and adopted by your audience.

# 1
# The Audience

et's begin by addressing the audience as our first component. Why? Because the audience is the most important of the three components of any presentation. Unfortunately, when we as presenters set about preparing to give a presentation, this is the component that gets the least attention. We spend virtually all of our time thinking about ourselves. What *we* want to tell the audience, what *we* think they need to know, what *we* want to talk about, what *we* think is important. If we do think about the audience at all, it's only to think about how nervous we're going to be getting up in front of them. In fact, that's how we think about the audience, as a "them." And often not a warm and fuzzy "them." We make them either unimportant or the object of our fear.

## Audience ≠ enemy

For some of us, the audience almost becomes an enemy, judging us, evaluating our clothing, critiquing our comedic skills. In fact, we believe that's why they're there. We spend hours awake at night imagining all the horrible thoughts our audience is bound to have about us when we stand in front of them to present. We begin by conjuring up their chuckles and sneers about our appearance. Then we move on to our presentation delivery. Surely they'll find us nervous, awkward, unfunny. Lastly we move on to thoughts of their response to our content. Boring, uniformed, or worse, inaccurate. We are absolutely positive that each audience member will sit as our judge and jury. Nothing could be further from the truth.

Frankly, the audience couldn't care less about us. They are like every fifteen-year-old you've ever known. They care only about themselves, and you matter to them only as far as you can do something for them. They have assembled to hear you speak because they have a need, a wish, a problem that needs fulfilling or solving. Your audience isn't there to evaluate your wardrobe or critique your performance skills. They haven't come for you at all. They've come for themselves. Your audience has come to hear what you have to say. They are planning, hoping, maybe even praying that what you are going to say will move them, change them, help them, make their lives easier, better, safer, richer, sexier, longer. What does every one of these thoughts have in common? Every single one of these thoughts is about THEM, not YOU. Okay, so it might pass through their minds for a second or two that they like or don't like your hair, your suit, your watch or your make-up, but ultimately their focus will be on your message. (Unless you're in the fashion or performance industry, they've not come with the purpose of even noticing what you look like.) Other than your message, you really have no meaning as far as they're concerned. Let me prove it to you. Just read the speech bubble at right.

And so it is. Audiences don't care whether there's a poppy seed in your teeth or your hair isn't perfect or you're not one bit funny. What they do care about is what's coming out of your mouth. Are you meeting their needs, showing them how to fulfill their wishes, addressing and solving their problems? They have paid a price —

not necessarily monetarily, but with their time (more valuable than money) and attention. The only thing they require of you is that you give them value in return. So how do you ensure that what you're saying will have value for them?

### Audiences Don't Care about Anything but Themselves: My Accidental Experiment

For years I've traveled up and down the East Coast giving my signature presentation, "Creating and Delivering Presentations That WOW and Win." At one point in the presentation (especially if it is one where a meal has just been served), I will ask the audience to imagine I have a piece of lettuce or a poppy seed stuck in my teeth. Then I say something like, "You'd look at me and think, 'Isn't it a shame, that nice woman is standing in front of all these people with a piece of food in her teeth.' And then you'd immediately turn to the person sitting next to you and ask, 'Do I have food in my teeth?' Because I have meaning for you only as I impact your life."

After a few months of saying this, I realized that I was wrong. They didn't turn to the person next to them. Instead, once I'd spoken the words, "a piece of lettuce or a poppy seed in my teeth," the audience would, without realizing they were doing it, pass their tongues over their own teeth, patrolling for rogue food particles stuck there. WITHOUT being aware of it, they were using me as a mirror for themselves. Of course they didn't care whether I had food in my teeth; the minute I mentioned the idea, they were immediately thinking about their own teeth. As a matter of fact, you may have just passed your tongue over your own teeth reading this. The content of this book matters to you only as it has meaning for you and your life. Am I right?

# Turn Your Focus 180°

You turn your focus 180°, that's how. Instead of thinking about yourself, about your appearance, your delivery, anything about YOU, you must turn your focus 180° and think about your audience. It means rather than thinking about what you want to tell them, you need to think about what they want and need to hear and how they will best hear it. Your focus should be all about them from the very beginning, starting when you're building your presentation right up to and including when you're giving it.

Imagine yourself sitting in the audience. Imagine you are one of them, with the same issues, needs, problems, backgrounds, knowledge. Never forget that perspective. It is this view of your presentation that matters. Before you begin creating a slide, before you hammer out an outline, you need to be sure you're developing it with the audience in mind. Your presentation should be built around them, not around you.

You are inviting them to hear you speak, much as you'd invite a guest to your home for cocktails or dinner. Wouldn't it be good to know their favorite beverages, whether they have any food allergies, their particular likes and dislikes? That kind of information would make for a better, more relaxed, more enjoyable event all around, wouldn't it? The same holds true for presentations. The more you can create it around your audience's tastes, the more enjoyable the process will be for all.

Understanding your audience is at the core of any successful presentation. In a sales presentation, or any presentation of a persuasive nature, your goal is to change hearts and minds. To convince your audiences to buy your product or adopt your initiative, it must matter to them. And you can know what matters to them only after you have given lots and lots of thought to them.

## Different Audience, Different Angle

Often we will have a specific goal for a presentation (especially a sales presentation), but how we get to that goal will be different for different audiences. For example, imagine you are persuading a five-year-old to take a certain action. Now imagine persuading a forty-five-year-old to do the same thing. No matter the desired outcome, you wouldn't use the same arguments for these two very different audiences. Say you're trying to convince the five-year-old to eat his vegetables. You'd probably suggest that eating broccoli will help him grow big and strong. Maybe you'd even bribe him with dessert. Now imagine getting the forty-five-year-old to eat his vegetables. He's already big and strong (and no longer five). How will you appeal to him? You may need to appeal to his desire for good digestion or his fear of cancer or his wish to be at an optimal weight.

Now imagine you gave no thought to your audience. You made the same "big and strong" argument to the forty-five-year-old, or made the "good digestion" argument to the five-year-old. How do you think those presentations would go over? Exactly.

And so it is when building presentations. One size rarely, if ever, fits all. Every audience has their own fears, needs, goals. It is these we must be thinking about. It is these things that must inform your presentation. Thus, you must always keep your focus turned 180°. You must put yourselves in the audience's shoes, sit yourselves in their seats, all the time, from the very beginning.

## When Does 180° Focus Begin?

When you are asked to present your product, service, idea, or concept to an audience, you should immediately start thinking about whom you'll be speaking to and learn about them. If you don't know much about your audience, you can ask a few questions of the person who invited you. If he or she can't help you, ask to be directed to someone who can. Don't be afraid of bothering someone or taking up his or her time. People love to help and they'll appreciate your interest in his or her audience.

# Assessing the Audience

At Bespeak, we use the Audience Assessment tool to learn as much as we can about our audience before we begin building our presentation. Feel free to use it, and add your own questions as well. Our assessment tool will serve as a good guideline for structuring your presentation. It will set you on the right path toward connecting with your audience, ensuring that you are addressing their needs, speaking their language, and creating maximum opportunity to be heard. We've included it here with explanations for each question. (There are directions at the end of this book for downloading a blank copy of the assessment.)

These questions will serve as a great starting point, but don't hesitate to develop your own. Every audience is different, as are goals for presentations. Experience will be a great guide as well. One presentation in front of one audience will alert you to questions you may want to ask before the next opportunity. Be aware of what you "wish you had known" about a particular past audience, and be sure to ask that question going forward. If you come upon questions you think we should include here, write to Bespeak to let us know!

# The Bespeak
# AUDIENCE ASSESSMENT TOOL

Read each question to see what it means in terms of your presentation planning, design, and implementation.

## WHO IS YOUR AUDIENCE? (PEERS, SUBORDINATES, SUPERIORS, CUSTOMERS, PROSPECTS, ASSOCIATION MEMBERS)

Answering this question will be an important step in developing a presentation that is driven by what matters to the members of your audience. You must address their needs, their problems, and their questions. You can do that only when you have a clear idea of who they are. The more information you can learn here, the better. If your presentation will be to a company, will you be presenting to the C-suite? Middle management? Everyone in the company? Is it a presentation to one department within the organization? More than one? How are these departments aligned? If you're presenting to a leaders' group, find out who they are, what kinds of companies they run, and what their issues are around your topic. If you're presenting at a large event (a conference or expo of some kind), information may be less specific. Still, you can get a good idea of what kinds of businesspeople attend — solo-preneurs and owners of small businesses or groups of people from specific departments in large companies? The answers to this question will help you develop a picture of who your audience will be and, thus, how you can best address their needs.

## How many will they be?

Will there be five attendees? Twenty-five? A hundred twenty-five? Mentally, you'll need to prepare for the number of people you will be talking to. This will help you structure time for Q and A (questions and answers), decide what type of visual aids to use, and it may influence the length and formality of your presentation. For example, if it is a smaller group, you can ask people before you begin your presentation what issues they may be experiencing that are connected to your topic. This is a great way to involve them immediately, let them know that addressing their concerns or problems is your primary objective, and that the presentation will be absolutely relevant to them. When I do this with a small group, I write each individual issue on a flip-chart page and tape it to the wall. Then, as we address each issue, I put a check mark next to it, showing that we've covered it.

When speaking to large groups, asking for questions at the beginning is not such a great idea. Unless you get answers from many audience members, it will be hard to know whether you've culled the issues of interest to everyone. You don't want to give a "boutique" presentation to a ballroom full of people. In addition, you run the risk of having forty hands raised and only four minutes to answer, or of having some long-winded person hi-jack your presentation. (This can happen in a small group as well, but is easier to control.)

Instead, with larger groups, make a point of letting people know how long you'll be speaking and that there will be time for questions at the end. I also add one caveat: I ask people to stop me mid-presentation if I say something they don't understand or about which they're confused. This ensures that I won't lose anyone along the way.

If I am speaking to a group larger than forty people, I usually use a PowerPoint presentation as a visual aid. I find a big visual gives a large audience something to connect with even when my gaze is not in the direction of a particular person or section.

## WHY ARE THEY COMING TO HEAR YOUR PRESENTATION? (EAGERLY, VOLUNTARILY, BY REQUIREMENT, UNDER PROTEST, WARILY, PESSIMISTICALLY)

Ideally, every audience member should be sitting on the edge of his or her seat in eager anticipation of your words of wisdom. In the real world you will have to deal with audience members who are skeptical at best and downright hostile at worst. Preparedness is your best defense. If you know why they're coming, you can come at them from the right angle. If they are attending under duress or coming with a pessimistic mindset, you can anticipate their objections and answer them before they're said out loud.

For example, when I speak to audiences that give presentations on a regular basis (salespeople), I speak to them as comrades. I know they're "in the trenches" every day. I also know where I'm going to get pushback (they typically don't like my suggestions about PowerPoint), and I let them know up front that they'll probably disagree with me. Then I drive my point home in a friendly, funny, but firm way.

On the other hand, if I'm speaking to an audience of novices or fearful speakers, I emphasize ways to conquer fear and to ensure confidence and a good experience. PowerPoint is the least of their worries, and I don't spend a lot of time discussing it.

## Do they know one another?

Is this a chummy group, or are they strangers to one another? The answer greatly indicates their behavior. If they know one another well, there's more likelihood of cross talk, a breakdown of order, and sabotaging. Philanthropic groups like Rotaries and Kiwanis clubs are notoriously lively. This can be a little unnerving if you're not prepared for it. Don't get me wrong — these are both terrific organizations filled with great people doing good works, but because they meet weekly, they know one another really, really well. This can lead to some good-natured (even hilarious) but rowdy behavior. Not exactly a presenter's most comfortable scenario, particularly when it comes as a surprise.

On the other hand, audience members who know one another will be less likely to ask questions, especially if the subject matter is supposed to be familiar to them. The reason is simple: they don't want to look stupid in front of their peers. In these situations you'll have to reward the brave askers. This will usually lead others to follow their lead.

The culture of the workplace or group is worth exploring as well. As you are asking questions of the person who invited you to speak, ask whether the group is friendly and how they usually behave during presentations.

In any organization or business, groups can be chummy and chatty or all pomp and circumstance. Knowing this ahead of time will bring huge payoffs in your comfort level.

Regardless of the group, you may get one Mr. Know-It-All or Mrs. Loves-the-Sound-of-Her-Own-Voice, or the self-appointed King or Queen of Comedy. These folks will interrupt, derail, and cause a ruckus, whatever the subject and whoever the presenter. Remember, you are not their sixth-grade teacher. Saying (with your arms folded), "Mr. Jones, would you care to share your obviously hilarious joke with the rest of the group?" is not a tactic you can implement here. You are the group's invited guest.

Your best defense when confronted with these potential sabotagers? SMILE. No kidding. Your smile indicates to your audience that you've got everything under control, even if what you really want to do is lose it altogether and dive across the table at Mr. Thinks-He's-So-Darned-Funny to wipe that smirk off his face permanently. It also indicates to whoever is loving the sound of his or her own voice that they have not ruffled your feathers in the least. Do not, however, allow them to steal your show. If he or she says something worthwhile, acknowledge it very briefly and then move on. If the call-out is just for laughs, smile and move on. If you can, stand near the disrupter and turn your attention to another part of the room. This should put a stop to the antics.

An audience of people who are strangers to one another is much less likely to interrupt or talk to a neighbor while you're talking. On the other hand, depending on the subject matter, you may get more questions from an audience of strangers who aren't worried about their neighbor's opinion and are freer to be themselves. If you know they'll be such a group, be sure to allow time for questions. Also, be sure to reward the first few questioners with praise for having asked their questions. A vibrant Q and A is always a great way to end a presentation, and your willingness to answer audience questions will endear you to them.

### IF THIS IS TO BE A PERSUASIVE PRESENTATION, ARE THE MEMBERS OF YOUR AUDIENCE THE ULTIMATE DECISION MAKERS, OR MUST YOUR IDEA BE RUN BY SOMEONE ELSE BEFORE A DECISION CAN BE MADE?

Do you need to create a buzz that will trickle up to the decision makers, or is that person in the room? If so, do some research and uncover his or her concerns, problems, and goals. Knowing the decision maker's "hot buttons" will help you create and deliver a presentation that does a great job of addressing his or her particular worries, needs, and desires.

Although it's important to know who the decision maker is, do NOT make the mistake of addressing only that person (or people) during your presentation. It's impolite, and more important, you've no way of knowing who has the decision maker's ear. He or she may want to hear the views of everyone attending about your idea or proposal before making a decision. Be sure everyone in the room feels that you connected with them. Why would you want it any other way? If they've been good enough to take the time to attend your presentation, you certainly want them to know you appreciate it. Decision maker or not, they are all valued audience members. (And by the way, you never know who'll be the next decision maker, either in this organization or another.)

## Is the audience at all familiar with your topic?

This may be harder to know. You can ask the event planner, manager, or administrator who hired you, send out a brief email, or (worst case) ask the audience before you begin. Be aware that if you choose the latter scenario, you risk losing control of the group right from the start. (Should this happen, simply remain silent until you have their attention. DO NOT shout over them, and don't frown.)

Often there are varying levels of knowledge about your topic. While you don't want to dumb it down too much, you do want to be sure you don't leave anyone behind. Trying to show off how much you know about your topic, using twelve-syllable words and unknown acronyms, is a sure way to make the unknowing masses seated before you feel stupid, and then angry. Not a way to build rapport.

If you feel insecure about your content, or if you think someone in the room may know as much or more than you do, get over it. DO NOT make the mistake of playing to Mr. Smarty Pants at the expense of the rest of the group. Majority rules when it comes to audiences. You have to speak to the greatest common denominator.

With that in mind, there is a way to get Mr. Smarty Pants on your side. Acknowledge him and his brain power early in your presentation. Saying something like, "As I'm sure my friend Ralph here probably knows . . . " will allow Ralph his moment in the sun without undermining your content or confusing others who have minimal knowledge of your topic. I've often gone even further and said, "If I should drop dead during this presentation, Ralph here can easily step in for me. He knows every bit as much about this stuff as I do." Now Ralph is just about crowing, blissful at having been acknowledged as an expert in this arena. He no longer needs to prove his prowess to the group, and I am free to go on speaking in a way the majority of the audience can understand, uninterrupted.

"Something for everyone" is a good motto with varied knowledge levels, but stay away from the higher levels of your expertise, at least until you get to Questions and Answers. At that time, if you get a brainiac asking a question, feel free to show him or her that you're a force to be reckoned with, but give a short definition or analogy if you can, to help those with more elementary knowledge not feel left out.

## IF THE AUDIENCE IS FAMILIAR WITH YOUR TOPIC, DO THEY HAVE ANY PRECONCEIVED NOTIONS YOU MAY NEED TO DISPEL?

This will be part of the brainstorming for your presentation. Once you know what their current state of mind is regarding your subject, you'll be better prepared to build your presentation. "The best defense is a good offense." You may not be able to forecast all their concerns, but knowing many of them will help you "bullet-proof" your argument. The best way to do that is to know what size and shape the bullets are, and where they're likely to be coming from.

If you know they're harboring misconceptions about your topic, you can tell them right off the bat that your goal is to disabuse them of these and illuminate the realities of —— (whatever it is). Perhaps some of their feelings are justified; acknowledge these. That will get their attention instantly because they'll see that you "get" where they're coming from.

**Help Me Avoid Being the Target of Tomatoes!**

A man came to me after one of my presentations with this problem: He was selling reverse mortgages, which had been (justifiably, according to him) getting a bad rap. He was aware of some of the shady things going on in this market segment and was afraid of being poorly received by the audiences he very much wanted to talk with about his product, which was a good one. I advised him to acknowledge these bad practices right up front, at the very beginning of his presentation. Get it out in the open and then explain why and how his product was different. You can't run from bad news or knowledge; you have to address it head on. By showing that he knew what the audience's thoughts were about reverse mortgages, he was able to connect with them and then show why his product was different.

## What's their level of interest?

Level of interest ties in to why your audience came and what reservations they may or may not have. Don't be dissuaded by a lack of interest. Maybe they don't know enough about your topic, or maybe they've been misinformed.

If you've been warned that your topic is not in the top five on their "need-to-know" list, you MUST begin your presentation by illustrating in a clear, concise, and convincing way why, in fact, it is important to them. This may take some thought on your part, and frankly, this is where most presenters fall short. When they're invited to present, they mistake it for an invitation to "pitch," seeing it as an opportunity to throw everything about their product or service at poor, usually captive, audience members.

You MUST first help your audience see their need for your product, service, or initiative before you tell them how it will fill that need. In other words, if there is no level of interest, you'd better create one, and make it big, compelling, and urgent.

## WHAT IS YOUR AUDIENCE'S ATTENTION SPAN?

For heaven's sake, if you're speaking to an organization or group that meets regularly and often has a speaker, stay within the allotted time frame! The same holds true when you're invited to pitch to a prospect or customer. Better yet, go short. No one ever faulted a presenter for being too brief. "Always leave them wanting more" is a great adage. It's never good to have people racing for the door as you're wrapping up, or yawning or checking their watches. If you can predict how long they'll be interested and engaged, don't push it.

The best predictors are: (1) how long you've been asked to speak and (2) if they've invited speakers before, how long those presentations have gone. Feel free to dig a little deeper with the person who invited you. Does the group prefer shorter or longer presentations? Would they rather have more time to socialize, more time for Q and A? Even if you are speaking to clusters of people within the same organization, or the same type of group in a different geographic area, this is research worth repeating.

## The Rare Exception

Every once in a while, however, this spokesperson is wrong. Years ago I spoke to a professional networking group. The man who invited me was so pessimistic about the audience's response to my topic that I literally tried to fire myself from the job, which was tricky because I wasn't being paid. He hemmed and hawed over the title, sighed and stammered about the possible turnout. "Well," he said to me, "if we're lucky, we'll get about fifteen people." And fifty showed up. It was NOT to see me (okay, there were three people there to see me). They showed up because they were interested in the topic. SO interested that I actually talked 10 minutes longer than I'd intended. What made me decide to "go long"? I could see on their faces, see in their postures, that they were hanging on every word. They wanted to hear more, so I gave it to them.

The moral of the story? Do your research beforehand, but always, always be light on your feet. If you start late and you know they have a hard stop at a certain time, you must shorten your remarks accordingly. If you see they are eagerly eating up what you're dishing out, give 'em more, but never more than five or ten minutes' worth. If they're interested in more than that, they'll invite you back!

## NAME FIVE REASONS YOUR TOPIC IS IMPORTANT TO THEM

These should be benefits, NOT features. They are things that matter to THEM. You may think something is important, but for them it's "Who cares?" Your five reasons are about them and only them. In fact, it's "Them 101"; it's "The World according to Them"; it's "All Them, All the Time." You get the idea. Once you've gathered all this information about your audience, you should be able to list these five reasons easily. Remember, the more compelling these benefits, the more irresistible your proposal, and the more opportunity for buy-in. Make it easy for them to say yes.

---

## Take Aways

- The audience is the most important component of any presentation.

- Audiences are there for themselves, not for you.

- Turn your focus 180°. Put yourself in the audience's seats.

- Different audiences require different angles.

- Use the Bespeak Audience Assessment tool before preparing for your presentation. It will help you gain clarity and insight about your audience.

Before you create an outline, open PowerPoint, or even brainstorm, you need to know as much as you can about the people coming to hear you speak. This knowledge will ensure that you craft a presentation that speaks in the language of your audience to their needs at their level of interest. Doing this work thoroughly will be well worth the effort. You'll be creating and delivering a message that gets heard and get results.

# 2
# The Message

Y ou've evaluated your audience, now you're ready to build your presentation. Although I believe every presentation is in some way persuasive, for the sake of goodwill, I'll allow that some presentations are informational. Whether persuasive or informational (or both), there are guidelines that should be followed for building every presentation.

## Bespeaking Their Language

Y ou've researched, studied, worked, breathed, and lived your topic, business, product, or service forever. You know it inside out and backward. It's complicated stuff, or at least it was at one time, but now all the terminology, acronyms, and initialisms (initials of words that, when put together, do not spell out a word; *FDIC* is an example of an initialism) are the language you speak, think, and dream. In fact, this language is plain English to you. You forget that it's actually a very specialized, particular language, maybe with its own arcane jargon, acronyms, and initialisms.

While you deserve a big pat on the back, kudos, and probably a raise for all you've learned, absorbed, and assimilated, you are not your audience. (The exception to this is if you are speaking to people in your industry, with your level of expertise. In that case, go have a blast using all your industry insider lingo. If not, heed this advice.)

### Bespeaking at their level

You MUST determine what your audience knows about your topic and speak to them on their level. Frankly, you may have to pretend they're eighth graders, or eight years old even, depending on your subject matter and their level of knowledge and comfort. (Not sure of their knowledge level? That's where the audience assessment comes in.)

I would suggest erring on the side of caution. Don't use acronyms or initialisms unless you're sure everyone in the room will know what they mean. If you catch an acronym flying out of your mouth, immediately follow it with its meaning. If you're using an uncommon word, define it right after you say it. (And please don't preface your definition with, "For those of you who don't know the meaning of this word . . . " That will sound condescending. Not a rapport builder.) If it's truly complicated, use an analogy to explain it. Analogies typically begin with "It's like . . ." or "Imagine that . . . ")

## Eliminate Babble-ing

At Bespeak, we use our Eliminate Babble-ing tool to help open presenters' eyes to the jargon, acronyms, and initialisms they're using every day. It's a very simple yet hugely effective tool. Here's an example of how it works. On the left side, jot down your industry's jargon words, acronyms, and initialisms. On the right side, write their definitions. You'll be astounded at how quickly you'll fill the page. (You'll find instructions on downloading your own copy at the end of this book.)

## Eliminate Babble-ing Worksheet

| My Industry's Acronyms, Initialisms, Jargon Words | Definitions |
| --- | --- |
| | |

Use the Eliminate Babble-ing worksheet as an eye-opener and language equalizer. Check every presentation against it to be sure you'll be speaking the audience's language.

## "What Is a Kilowatt, Anyway?"

Years ago I worked with the CT Clean Energy Fund (now the Clean Energy Finance and Investment Authority), a terrific organization that promotes and helps provide clean energy throughout the state of Connecticut. One of my tasks for the company was to edit its PowerPoint decks.

Slide after slide talked about "kilowatts." It was 30 kilowatt this and 180 kilowatt that. So, I built a slide that was a cartoon of a light bulb and above it the question, "What is a kilowatt, anyway?"

When I showed the slide, one of the guys, an engineer, said, "That's easy. A kilowatt is a thousand watts." To which I responded, "Look, if you don't want to tell me what it is, just say so." Telling me a kilowatt is a thousand watts did nothing to advance my understanding of a kilowatt (or a watt for that matter). A helpful answer would be, "With a kilowatt, you can run your dishwasher for three days." If he were presenting to students, a better definition would be, "With a kilowatt, you can play your Gameboy for a week." Those examples would be useful ways of helping me (and his audience) understand the concept.

Remember, think about your audience. Make sure you're speaking a language they understand.

### The awful unintended consequence of babble-ing

You must be speaking the audience's language because if you don't, you won't get your message across. Unlike children, grown-up audiences will not raise a hand and ask for clarification. They'll simply start checking their Blackberries and iPhones.

Worse, the more terminology an adult audience doesn't understand, the more they will feel "stupid." And feeling stupid not only feels bad, it has an awful ricochet effect. It goes something like: "I feel stupid. Feeling stupid feels bad. Who made me feel stupid? You did! Now I feel bad about you!" You never, ever want audiences to feel bad about you. You want them to feel good about you, and, more important, good about your message. Thus you must be speaking in a language they can hear and understand.

## Make difficult concepts accessible

While it's easy to take acronyms and initialisms out of your presentation, if the entire concept is over the audience's head, your job is more difficult and more imperative. More often than not, when I'm helping a client build a presentation, he or she will insist, "But I have to tell them this." The *this* is typically some hugely technical piece of information that makes the presenter look like Super Smarty Pants, but does nothing to (a) make the presenter's real point or (b) increase the audience's understanding. In fact, often the *this* is something important to the presenter but NOT to the audience. Even worse, many presenters fill their presentations with all kinds of *this*es that increase their Smarty Pants quotient but leave their audiences bored or confused, or both. *This*es like these do not a successful presentation make.

You MUST figure out a way to explain important concepts in a way your audience can understand. This requires time and more time and lots of thought. (And running it by an eight- or eighty-eight-year-old wouldn't hurt.) No matter the time or amount of energy needed, it must be done. If the audience isn't going to get it, what's the point? The good news is, it will be time and energy well spent. Once you have the analogy or simple example figured out, you can use it over and over.

If you know your topic is complicated, start now thinking about ways to "dumb it down." Run your ideas by regular people, people NOT associated with your industry. When the eight- or eighty-eight-year-old gets it, you know you've got a winner.

Nail It.

---

## Take Aways

- Watch for acronyms and jargon words.

- If you inadvertently use one of the above, define it!

- Use analogies to help explain difficult concepts.

- Run the presentation by an industry or department outsider to be sure it's understandable.

# Words Matter

Not only do you want to avoid filling your presentation with jargon words, acronyms, and initialisms, you want to beware of using what I call weak, wishy-washy words. These are words that cut you off at the knees, diminish your stance, and undermine your argument. Here are some of the worst offenders.

## Weak, Wishy-Washy Words

### *Try*

No one pays anyone to *try*. They pay people to succeed. Imagine if a pilot came on the airplane's speaker system and said, "Good afternoon, folks. In just a few minutes we're going to be getting under way to *try* to get you to Houston." I can hear safety belts unbuckling and passengers stampeding to the door. Trying doesn't count. DOING counts. Tell audiences what you do or intend to do, or what your proposed solution will do, not what you'll *try* to do.

### *Strive*

The sneaky stepsister of *try*. See above. Abandon word.

### *Hopefully*

If you've put your heart and soul into something — an event, an argument, a product or service, your own education and development — there's no need to *hope* they will like, appreciate, adopt, or hire it or you. You must speak completely confidently. It's not, "*Hopefully,* everything's going well for you at the conference today," or "*Hopefully,* you'll get something out of this presentation today," or "*Hopefully,* what I'm saying is making sense." These sentences give the audience the impression that you've got your fingers crossed, you're wishing on a star, shaking the Magic Eight Ball, or consulting a Ouija board.

*Hopefully* does nothing to instill confidence in you, your expertise, or your product or service.

Instead, say, "We trust you're having a great experience at today's event." Or, "I'm completely confident you'll take away valuable information from my presentation today." Plant both feet firmly in the positive.

### Sort of/kind of

The words *sort of* and *kind of* are meant to introduce an analogy (think, "it's like") to illustrate two things that are akin to each other in some way or to say maybe. These days they're incorrectly used all the time before an explanation of something that stands alone, is not being compared to another thing, and is absolutely definitely what it is. Example: "We're *sort of* a software development company," or "We're *kind of* expanding into the European market." Huh? Are you a software development company or not? Are you expanding into the European market or not? These are straightforward statements that should be unequivocal or not stated at all.

### Assist

Yawn. *Assist* is what you do to help a little old lady across the street — NOT what you do in the dynamic world of business. Replace this totally unsexy sleep-inducing verb with *partner* (who doesn't want a partner?) or the never-out-of-style *help*.

### Interface

Okay, I'll admit I dislike this word because it reminds me of seventh-grade home economics class. (We made skirts. On "modeling day" mine was held together mostly with safety pins . . .) Facing is the material that goes in-between two other fabrics. To interface is to go between two things. Unless you're talking about two computers communicating with each other, *interface* has no place in your vocabulary. Human beings don't *interface;* they connect! They meet! They talk, make decisions, argue, negotiate. You get the idea.

### *Just*

As in, "We're *just* a little software company" or "I *just* want to talk for a minute about . . ." or "I *just* want to thank . . ." You're not *just* a little software company. (And take out the word *little* while you're at it.) Nor do you *just* want to talk for a minute, or "just thank." Talking and thanking are full-blown activities, neither of which requires a qualifier, diminisher, or hedger. The fix for this is simple: eliminate the *just*.

### *You guys*

Unless you are addressing a room that is exclusively male, please, please, do not address them as *you guys*, and even then only if it's a casual affair. (If they're in suits or tuxedos, I'd suggest addressing them as gentlemen.) *You guys* is casual slang. Ick.

These words are just a handful and, in my opinion, some of the worst offenders. Watch your language; eliminate these weak, wishy-washy words from your presentations. They're hurting the force and power of your argument. They're diminishing your impact as a presenter. Wipe them out of your vocabulary. And when you do, you can replace them with BIG, BOLD, BRAVE words.

## Big, Bold, Brave Words

Here are some words I LOVE. These words are the antithesis of weak, wishy-washy words. These are words that evoke good feeling. They're uplifting, powerful, and positive. Equally important, these are words that an eight-year-old or an eighty-eight-year-old can understand. That's the thing about great words. They don't require a dictionary or thesaurus or a master's degree, just a knowledge of basic English and a beating heart.

Below are only a few of many. You can absolutely add your own to this list.

Nail It.

### Create

Just saying this word makes me feel good. We are all looking for ways to be creative or help with the creation of something.

### Empower

Okay, this is one of those words that was so overused a few decades ago it was "out." I LOVE it. I think it says exactly what it means. If you, your idea, or product or service empowers others, by all means shout it to the rafters.

### Excel

Not the Microsoft product or the sports center. Do you excel at something? Does your idea? Your product? Don't be shy. Let your audience know.

### Expand/grow

The only things we don't want to expand or grow is our waistlines or our debt.

### Partner

Say this instead of *assist.*

### Enhance

A prettier way of saying "make better."

### Double, triple

If you improve things measurably, say so. And round it off, will ya? Don't tell them 52%, just say 50% or half. They will get the idea. Actually, they will get the idea better when you round off the numbers.

### *Terrific, spectacular, wonderful*

We all know and use these words in everyday conversation; in business, not so much. Why not? These are juicy, expressive words. And you're giving a presentation specifically to express something: yourself, an idea, an initiative, the benefits of a product or service. Use real, expressive words like these!

### *Critical, crucial, key*

All these words speak to necessity, urgency. Speakers are afraid to use these kinds of words because they're so strong — exactly why you should use them.

These are only a sampling of big, bold, brave words. I'm sure you can think of plenty on your own. You, too, can become a word nerd. Start paying attention to those you find most compelling. Whose comments at a meeting or in a presentation pack the biggest punch? What words are they using? My bet is that they're using words that connect, words that inspire, words that evoke feelings, that ignite the senses. Go ahead and try on a few of them. If they feel awkward or false, abandon them. If they feel good, if they make you smile, if there's a kind of "zing" going from the tip of your toes to the top of your head, you're there. You're using words that give you as much energy as they give the audience. BINGO.

## Take Aways

- Beware of weak, wishy-washy words. Eliminate them from your vocabulary.

- UP your use of BIG, BOLD, BRAVE words. Discover some of your own.

- Don't be afraid to use real, juicy, everyday words. These words move people.

# Structuring Your Presentation

Okay, now that we've addressed words, let's look at structure. We'll start with the basics; a simple structure you can use in any and every presentation. It involves the rule of threes. It's a rule I believe in so strongly, I refer to is as magic.

## The Magic Rule of Threes

I am a firm believer in the magic rule of threes. Three strikes and you're out; the genie gives the lucky lampholder three wishes; Goldilocks and the three bears; beginning, middle, and end; morning, noon, and night; stop, yield, and go; yes, no, and maybe; Larry, Mo, and Curly; me, myself, and I . . . the list goes on and on.

What does this have to do with presentations? Everything! People love threes. They're easy to listen to and (more important) to remember. When you begin your presentation by telling the audience, "I'm here today to talk about three main things," or "There are three reasons why this system works," you can almost see them relax. Why? They know they can hold on to three ideas. Three ideas will not strain or tax their minds. Plus, we have all grown up with threes; our minds naturally gravitate toward the idea of grouping things that way.

### Beginning, middle, and end

As you prepare your presentation, plan around the rule of threes. First of all, every presentation should have a beginning, middle, and end. How many presentations have you seen that sort of end without an ending? You're left holding a group of ideas without anything to tie them together. You've probably heard this before, but the simple structure of: "Tell 'em what you're going to tell 'em, tell 'em, and then tell 'em what you told 'em" is well known because it works.

What do I mean by using the magic rule of threes in your presentation? It means organizing it with three main points, three problems, three goals or three periods of time. For example, a sales (or other persuasive presentation) can be built around the three main problems the audience has that your idea, product, or service will solve. A presentation to a board of directors can apply the rule of threes chronologically: here's where we were, here's where we are now, here's where we're going.

And for heaven's sake, don't make more than three main points. What if you have more than three points to make? I urge you to take a close look at your presentation to see where you can pare it down. Typically, we mislabel our main points or include something that doesn't belong or we say the same thing but in a different way. Be a tough editor and stick to three. I am absolutely unyielding about this, and with good reason.

---

**When It Comes to Benefits, the Magic Number Is Five**

I will admit, there are those who advocate having five "benefits" in a sales presentation. As militant as I am about the magic rule of threes, this I will allow. Why? Well, the reasoning is that if you give the audience five benefits of your project or service in a sales presentation, they can throw two out and still be left with (drum roll, please) three! Voila! By giving them five benefits, you cast your net a little wider, but not so wide that you lose or overwhelm your audience. So, when it comes to benefits of your product or service, think five. When it comes to anything else in your presentation, the lucky number is (say it with me now) three.

---

## Brain overload = audience lost

Think of the last time you listened to a sermon given by a priest, minister, or rabbi. There you are, sitting in your place of worship, intently listening. He makes his first point, and it's a good one; second point, you're right there with him. Third point, he's still got you. When he makes his fourth point, you sit up a little taller and take a deep breath; you really want to stay with this guy. Now he makes the fifth point and you're really hoping for the conclusion. Your brain is full. Unfortunately, he goes on to make point number six; now he's gone beyond what you can retain. You drop all of what he's said from your short-term memory and STOP LISTENING. Instead, you start focusing on what you're going to pick up at the grocery store on your way home. Worse, you might even feel a little angry, and justifiably so. This speaker took you outside the boundaries of what you (and most of his audience) could reasonably retain. All that effort wasted. On a Sunday (or Friday night or Saturday), maybe not such a big deal. On a weekday in a boardroom for a big sales presentation, it's a really big deal.

So do yourself and your audience a favor. Structure your presentations around the rule of threes. Your audience will remember you, and your content. What's more, they will have enjoyed listening to you because you made the experience successful for THEM.

# Stories

While we're on the subject of threes and building your presentation, let's talk about storytelling. Storytelling in a presentation is great for a number of reasons. First, we all, no matter our age, love a story. People have been telling stories since they learned to communicate. In a presentation, it's the story that drives the point home, gives it fabric and texture, and makes your point stick.

You can use stories in several different ways. A story can create connection, illustrate an idea, or prove a point.

### Create connection

If you've traveled out of town to make your presentation, you can tell a story about your travel to get there (provided it's either funny, inspirational, or complimentary of the location). If you're speaking to an audience with whom you share an expertise or profession, you can tell a story related to that — perhaps something new in your field of work, a conversation you had with one of them the night before, how you got interested in this topic. You can also tell a complimentary (feel-good) story about the person who introduced or invited you. These kinds of stories allow you to speak casually, authentically, in a warm natural way. These kinds of stories create a connection between you and your audience.

### Illustrate an idea

Particularly if your subject matter is confusing or abstract, telling a story can be a great way to provide clarity. You can use an analogy (begin with, "It's like . . ."), but make sure it is truly an accurate comparison. This may take some time to create, but it will be well worth it. When you come up with a killer story that clearly communicates a complicated concept, you have struck gold. Why? Because everyone remembers stories. Telling a story that illustrates your point makes your point sticky. Brilliant.

Nail It.

## Prove a point

If stories are sticky, when you're proving your point you absolutely want to use stories to drive your point home. Each story you tell should lead to one of two conclusions: either showing the great good things that happen when your point is agreed to or the bad, awful things that happen when it's not. I'm always a fan of the carrot (good) rather than the stick (bad), but I'll leave this one up to you.

The layout of the story would look like this: there was a problem or goal, you implemented your solution (idea / product / service) and produced a great result. The "stick" story would be this: there was this problem or goal, your solution was not implemented (perhaps someone else's solution was implemented), and this produced a NOT great result. Either way, you're using a story to give weight to your argument. The story sticks, as does your point.

## Again, have a beginning, middle, and end

No matter what kind of story you're telling or what your purpose, every story must have a beginning, middle, and end. The story begins at the starting point: a journey, a decision to be made, a problem or goal. Then in the middle there is a crossroads, a decision made, a solution. The end is the lesson learned, a result, a conclusion reached.

# Bad Storytelling

While we all tell stories every day all the time, some of us do it better than others. Here are three examples of bad storytelling. Do you see yourself or someone you know in any of these?

## The revolving door

This is the story that has a beginning, middle, and end, but then goes right back to the beginning, middle, and end, and then right back . . . You get the idea. The teller goes around and around and around until all you want to do is catch her at the end of one of her revolutions and pull her OUT of this endless retelling. Tell your story once, include all three parts in order, and be done.

## The road to nowhere

This is the story that goes on and on. For the life of you, you can't figure out what the point of it is. The teller starts talking, and then he talks some more, and then he talks some more, and at some merciful point stops talking, but what he talked about is anybody's guess. Where did the story actually begin? What was the critical moment? What was its conclusion? Nobody knows.

## The cliffhanger

This kind of story has a beginning, and possibly even a compelling middle, but we never learn how it all turns out. The teller stops talking or moves on to something else, and we're left hanging. Minutes tick by with the presenter's mouth moving, but we hear nothing. In our minds we see "?" We're still stuck on the story, wondering how in the world it ended. This is particularly detrimental in a persuasive presentation. Ideally we want to tell stories that illustrate how we SOLVED a problem and what the result of our solution was. Plenty of people claim to have solutions, but do these solutions lead to the desired result? This third part is critical.

When I started my business, I attended a weekly networking meeting where we all stood and gave our sixty-second speeches about our businesses. One of the gentlemen in the group regularly shared with us a problem one of his clients was facing. Then he sat down. He hadn't said what his solution to the problem was, nor how his solution benefited his client. Audience baffled; opportunity wasted.

Nail It.

## And one more thing . . .

NO matter what, DON'T lie. (I don't believe in lying, period, but especially when telling a story.) Don't make up an ending, a situation, a circumstance. You may want to change a name or not divulge too much for the sake of someone's privacy or propriety. That's fine, and smart thinking. But NEVER try to put one over on your audience. You're bound to get caught, and then your credibility is out the window.

### A Cautionary Tale

I saw a business consultant give a presentation a few years ago, and I couldn't put my finger on a real reason, but the guy turned me off. About a month later I was talking to a colleague, and he mentioned having seen the same guy giving a presentation and his own negative impression. "What really bugged me was that he told this story in the first person, as though it had happened to him, and I had just read the exact same story in a book on marketing. In fact, when he got to the punch line, I said it out loud with him. Really embarrassed the guy. What a jerk."

The sad part of this story is that the presenter would have been every bit as effective if he'd told the story and credited the author, or the book, or even said, "I just read this great story . . ." Then my friend would have been nodding his head in agreement, having read the story himself. This would have created a bond between presenter and audience. Instead, it destroyed the speaker's credibility. My friend could only think, "If he lied about something as simple as this, what else would he lie about?"

## Take Aways

- Use the magic rule of threes in your presentations; create three labeled "mind buckets" into which your audience can put the information you're giving them.

- If you think you have more than three main points, take a good, hard look at your content. Does everything belong?

- Use stories to connect, illustrate, and prove a point.

- Don't be a bad storyteller: no revolving doors, roads to nowhere or cliff-hangers!

Remember, stories are powerful when told effectively and honestly. (And please, please don't forget to tell us how it ends!)

# Persuasive Presentations

believe every presentation is a persuasive presentation. What's more, I believe we spend most of our waking hours in persuasive communication. Think about it, you start the day convincing your teenager to get out of bed, into the shower, and out the door in time to make the bus. You persuade a co-worker to go to an Indian rather than Italian restaurant for lunch. You persuade your boss to let everyone take a half day on Fridays from Memorial Day to Labor Day. You persuade your sales team to stay up late to practice an upcoming presentation; you persuade your grade-schooler to finish her homework before going out to play; and as the day ends, you persuade your husband to have dinner with your family this weekend. Whew! I'm pooped just thinking about all this persuading (and kudos to you for your success at it). We are all trying to persuade others all the time. Presentations are simply group persuasion, and usually for higher stakes than, say, Indian food vs. Italian. Even if your presentation feels more informative than persuasive, it's a good idea to persuade the listeners to pay attention by explaining why your topic has meaning for them.

## Introducing the Bespeak Persuasive Presentation Format

So the question becomes, how do we construct the most compelling, convincing, persuasive presentation? At Bespeak, we use a structure for persuasive presentations developed by organizational psychologist Dr. Michael Grimes. Time and again, this simple, straightforward outline has proved itself in industries of all kinds, shapes, and sizes. It begins with an explanation of the audience's line of thought.

## What's the audience thinking?

Research shows that audience members usually think along similar lines regardless of what presenters are saying to them. As they listen, their thoughts go something like this:

1. What is the main point of the presentation?

2. Why should I pay attention?

3. What do you want me to consider?

4. What are the benefits to me if I do?

5. What about my concerns with "X" (your point)?

6. What support is there for your approach?

7. What exactly does this amount to?

8. What are the next steps to take if I'm interested?

As you prepare your presentation, keep these questions in mind. In other words, each step of the way, put yourself in your audience members' shoes. If you're not getting it or not buying it, chances are they won't either. Conversely, if you're excited about what you're reading and you're finding it convincing and compelling, they will too. (Before you begin mapping out the presentation itself, you need to know to whom you will be presenting. See Audience Assessment tool in chapter 1.)

## The design format

Use the following model to design your presentation. Each part of this model follows the audience's line of thought. Your finished product will follow the path an audience member takes when listening, making it that much easier for your message to be processed and adopted easily.

(Find instructions for downloading this template at the end of this book.)

# The Bespeak
## PERSUASIVE PRESENTATION FORMAT

### POINT

Write down the main point of your presentation in one sentence. Read it back to yourself as though you were reading it to your audience. Is it easily, immediately understood? Compelling? Of sincere interest to them? If the answer to any of these questions is no, rephrase your main point to speak CLEARLY and DIRECTLY to their interest.

Your point is not necessarily something you will say to them flat out. It is used primarily to help you frame the content of your presentation. This may seem like the easiest, most obvious part of building a presentation, but if I had a nickel for every client who has looked at me doe-eyed and dumbfounded when asked the question, "What's the main point of this presentation?" . . . Best to figure this out at the beginning.

### PICTURE

Here we draw a "picture" of what's going on in the world of the audience. It could be the world as a whole, the world of their industry, their company, their department. It could be the world of parenthood, retirement, divorce. Whatever it is, the crucial part of this picture is your illustration of the biggest problem, threat, or (conversely) aspiration faced by your audience and which your solution will address and solve. This is where you spell out the problem they're facing or the goal they're trying to achieve. Let your audience know you're on their wavelength; you've put yourself in their shoes (or better yet, you've been in their shoes); you're well versed in their problem; and (good news!) you have the solution. Keep in mind that you may have to inform them of their current urgent problem. It may be one of which they are unaware.

The idea here is to let them know you know where they are, what matters to them, and what they're worried about. Your goal is to have heads nodding here. "Yeah, exactly," they should be thinking. "She gets exactly where I am/we are." You are pulling your "presentation train" out of the station and you want everyone on board. Painting their picture creates a connection and a willingness to get on board with you and see where you'll take them.

## PROPOSAL

Recommend your solution to their common problem. Describe your solution or idea so that it is easily and quickly acceptable to the audience. It should be something they can understand and implement. They should be able to see immediately that it will enhance their "picture," solve their problem, or get them to their goal.

Talk about your proposal in compelling language that will resonate with them. Be careful not to use your own industry jargon and acronyms. You do not want to lose them at this critical juncture. This is where their hearts become light with anticipation of implementing your solution. The joy it will bring! The peace of mind!

## PAYOFF

And as they begin thinking of sugar plums and lollipops, you outline benefits for them. Indicate in order of importance the great good things the listener will receive when he or she implements or adopts your proposal. Spell it out. By benefits, I mean ways in which your solution will make their lives better, easier, richer, less stressful, less complicated, give them more time, more freedom, more happiness, more security, more stability, more profit . . . Get the idea? This is not about bells and whistles. It's about what those bells and whistles do for the listener.

## PROOF

Anticipate audience objections at this point, and have your rebuttals well thought out and ready. Anecdotes will be particularly helpful here. Brainstorm the "What about's" and the "What if's" in advance. The more able you are to answer these objections, the more you bulletproof your idea. Your thorough audience assessment will give you the ability to predict what size and shape these bullets will be and from where they'll be coming.

## POSITIONING

Restate the current situation of your audience, your solution, and the benefits of adopting it. This is the "taking stock of where you've come thus far" moment. It gives the audience a chance to take another look at everything you've said and to see how it all comes together.

## Prompt

Call for action on their part. Request some step to be taken immediately, before they leave the site of the presentation, if possible. Even a pledge taken with a raised hand can have significant results. If that is not possible, make sure they know the next step(s) to take. If you've done a good job with the other elements of this formula, they will be ready and eager for you to tell them what to do next. "So, now what?" they're thinking. Tell them. This is the last part of your persuasive presentation. DO NOT omit it!

From here you open things up for questions. As that ends, thank your audience again for having you.

# Putting the Bespeak Format To Work: A Real-Life Example

Let's say I'm a lover of "chick flicks" (romantic comedies and teary dramas), and my husband's a guy who loves (as he calls them) "car crash movies." If it doesn't have a car crash in it, he's not so interested in seeing it. There's a new chick flick movie I'm eager to see, but how to get my husband to come along? I could walk into the den and say, "There's a chick flick I want to see starting in twenty minutes. Get your coat," but chances are I wouldn't get the result I'm looking for. I'd be smarter (and more successful) using the Bespeak Persuasive Presentation format, which would go something like this:

**Me:** Hey, honey, you know how the last three movies we've seen have been car crash movies and you said next time we saw a movie it would be my turn to pick? And you know how you really don't like seeing my kind of movies? (Picture)

**Husband:** (hesitantly acknowledging) Yeah?

**Me:** Well, there's my kind of movie playing in town, and I'd like to go see it tonight, and I think you'll really enjoy yourself. (Proposal)

**Husband:** Really? (He's curious now.)

**Me:** Yep, I do. It is more of a chick flick, but it's got a car crash in it, and it's got one of your favorite action guys as the leading man. I was thinking if we go to the five o'clock show we could go to that little seafood restaurant you love afterward. (Payoff)

**Husband:** OK, but ...

**Me:** I know, I know. The last chick flick we went to was a real bummer, and I know how you hate unhappy endings. This one has gotten rave reviews. Both Tony and Bob loved it — and you know how they hate anything girly — and I know for a fact it ends happily. (Proof)

**Husband:** Really ...

**Me:** Yep! I think it's a no-brainer. We both agree it's my turn to pick a movie, and this one's got a car crash and an action hero in it for you, PLUS I'm throwing in dinner at your favorite seafood place afterward. What have you got to lose? (Positioning)

**Husband:** Nothing, I guess.

**Me:** Exactly! Grab your coat! I want to get some popcorn — with lots of butter for you — before the coming attractions. (Prompt)

And that's how easy it is to implement our format into any persuasive presentation you're giving. Draw the audience a picture of what's going on in their lives, complete with the problem your solution will solve. Give them your proposal for solving this problem. Tell them the payoff — what's in it for them. Prove that your proposal will indeed work by overcoming their objections even before they have a chance to say them out loud. Position yourself for success by quickly reviewing the path you've just taken them on, and, finally, prompt them to commit to or perform the logical next step.

# The Bespeak Presentation Method and the Rule of Threes

All persuasive presentations come down to the following three things:

problem

solution

result

This, my dear presenter, is the holy trinity of persuasive presentations.

First, you must know, understand, and be able to clearly and "pain-makingly" articulate your audience's problem. Put yourself in their seats. Turn your focus 180°. What is the burning, pressing problem that's keeping them up at night (or should be)? What issue are they struggling with? What new technology or government ruling or economic status has brought this particular problem to "critical" status?

**Finding the Problem So You Can Provide the Solution**

Sometimes you have to create the problem or remind your audience of one they may not have been aware of. A few years back, absolutely everything was "social media" and Web 2.0. You couldn't swing a dead cat without hitting someone speaking about those topics. What's more, everyone and their brother wanted to hear the expert speak. For a minute or two, I felt a little worried. Were sales presentations becoming obsolete? Were people not going to learn about ways to give them correctly? Was I about (gulp) to be a dinosaur?

Not a chance. I thought about it for a day or two and decided on a new introduction for my solution: my presentation, "Great Presenters and Presentations: Separating Fact from Fiction." Here's how the new intro went: "You've twittered and facebooked; you're linked in and plaxoed. All of these new media are great and wonderful. All of it is (hopefully) drawing prospects to your website, but at some point, depending on your business, you are still going to have to get in front of that prospect and present your product or service. Let's talk about the best ways to do that." Thus, I had created the need for my solution: my road show.

# Problem-Solution-Result

A nd so should you begin each of your presentations. Start by illustrating for your audience their problem: the WHY, the "what's wrong," the thing that's nagging at them, preventing them from having a good night's sleep.

Then you give them your solution. The HOW. Here's how you're going to solve their problem, fix the thing that's wrong, enable them to sleep through the night. (This is your product or service.) Step one, you shine the light on the need. Step two, you offer your solution.

Step three is the result. The WHAT. What will happen to them once they adopt your solution? What will the outcome be? How will their lives be better, safer, easier? How will their businesses be more efficient, successful, enduring?

### Sales Presentations

The majority of sales presentations I've been subjected to (no offense) begin with long bios of those presenting, followed by an extensive look at the history of the seller's company, followed by an explanation in minute, painstaking detail of the product or service the seller provides.

You know what the prospect is thinking during all this? "Who cares?" Salespeople take note: your prospects have invited you to speak to them because you've given them some indication you can solve their problem. Start by talking about that. Finish by talking about yourselves. Use the history of your company as part of your proof: that you've been around long enough, had enough experience with people like them and problems like theirs to know that you can absolutely solve their problem as well. Don't forget: you matter to them only as much as you positively affect them. Follow the Bespeak Persuasive Presentation format. You'll get the sale.

Let these magic threes — problem-solution-result — be your guide in all your persuasive presentations. Plug them into the Bespeak format and you'll be winning every time. (And getting to see the movies you love with your own loved one.)

---

## Take Aways

- Use the Bespeak Persuasive Presentation method to format your persuasive presentations.

- Remember to think problem-solution-result.

- For sales presentations, abandon your "All about Us" intro and begin instead by talking about the prospect's PICTURE (Problem).

- Talk about yourself at the end as PROOF that you can deliver on your proposal.

# 3
# Visual Aids

Now that you've got your presentation built, you may or may not need visual aids to accompany it, and they may or may not be PowerPoint slides. You need to take a long, hard, objective look at your subject and your audience to determine whether visuals will truly be an aid. Often, we are compelling enough, and any visual other than ourselves will only divert the audience from us and the power of our message.

Ideally, every visual aid, no matter the type, should be a synergistic component of your presentation. It, plus you, should equal much more than either could alone. It should illuminate your point in ways that you alone — no matter how many words you use in whatever amazing order — cannot, or at least in a way that is equally if not more compelling.

## Please, no reading!

Visuals are also helpful because some of us take in information through our eyes more readily than our ears. Delivering your point in both ways then widens your net.

That said, eyes and ears do not receive information in the same way. It does NOT aid your audience to give them visuals that are text-intensive. Why? Because we read and listen from the same side of our brains. Thus, when you show slides that have lots and lots of text, you are also presenting your audience with a terrible choice: do they want to read or do they want to listen? They cannot do both at the same time. Is that really a choice you want to present them with? Of course not. And for those of you thinking, "I'll solve this! I'll read the slide to them." First, THEY CAN READ. Second, they can read somewhere between three to ten times faster than you can speak, and besides, THEY CAN READ.

Ideally, we want them to look at something (a chart or diagram) while we explain its importance. We want to use a visual to help us illustrate something to make what we are saying clearer. We may want to use a photograph to help evoke an emotion. No matter what, we want our visuals to be a synergistic component, not a competing one.

---

# Good visuals show. They don't tell.

At Bespeak, we say every visual aid should have the "Huh?" factor. In other words, the audience should look at the visual and think, "Huh?" because the total meaning of the visual is unclear. The audience will then look to the presenter to explain it. This is why charts and graphs, laid out the right way (and easily seen from the back row) are effective visuals. You can show a line chart, bar graph, or dots on a map and know that the audience will look to you for explanation.

And since you are there, live and in person, to explain the bar chart, pie chart, or line graph, you can keep the visuals stripped down and simple. You do NOT need sentences of text above, below, or to the sides of the chart to explain to them in minute detail what they're looking at. That's why YOU are there.

### Think billboard, not dictionary

Any kind of text on a visual should be BIG, BOLD, and BRIEF. No more than five words per bullet, no more than five bullets per slide (three is ideal for both). Your font size should be no smaller than sixteen points for chart labeling. All bulleted text should be no smaller than a twenty-point font.

Right about now you're probably shaking your head. Most of what you've read thus far has been relatively easy to swallow, but five words on a bullet! Three bullets on a slide! "C'mon," I hear you thinking, "Get real." Oh, and the strings of words on each bullet should have the "Huh?" factor as well. In other words, if you sent the PowerPoint presentation to the audience, they would not be able to figure out the content of your message. Their curiosity would be piqued, but they would absolutely need you to explain what they were looking at.

Now take a minute or two to think back to the most recent presentations you have attended. If the presenter threw up screen after screen of bulleted text-filled slides, I'm betting you either: (1) read the slides and ignored the speaker, (2) ignored the slides and listened to the speaker, or (3) heaved a heavy sigh and played with your Blackberry or iPhone. Am I right? Now, think back to a presentation you attended where the speaker used either no slides, or very few with hardly any text and great, easy-to-see, relevant visuals. What was that experience like? Ahhhh, now you're getting it. And, by the way, when did we ever start thinking that slides were a replacement for your own notes, and that those notes would be appropriate, useful visual aids for your audience?

## Visuals should aid the audience, not the presenter

Thirty years ago, if you wanted a sophisticated visual aid, you put slides in a carousel tray and "clicked" through them as you talked. This was done recreationally, as in, "Here we are on our trip to the Grand Canyon," or educationally, as in, "What you're looking at here is an amoeba," or professionally, as in, "As you can see from this slide, earnings have increased 22% since last year." You were looking at a picture or diagram. I'd venture to say you were never looking at bullet points.

Fast forward to today. PowerPoint "slides" are used by presenters worldwide to display their written content to their audiences. When did we come to think of this kind of visual as an aid (to the audience, I mean)? We have all been the audience, and we all know how mind-numbingly boring such presentations are. In fact, the only thing we usually remember from a presentation where the only visuals were screen after screen of lots and lots of words is how bored we were watching it.

Presenters cling to their "decks" full of words the way a terrified speaker grips the podium. Talk to them of replacing these visuals with images, graphs, charts, or great evocative photos, and they respond with, "But what will I have to remind myself what to say next?" To them (and you) I say this: Would you expect an actor, even in a staged reading of a play, to display the script, even an abbreviated version, for the audience? Of course not. What would be the point of watching the actors when you could just as easily read the script yourself?

Why should a presentation be any different? Why would the audience want to read what you're about to say? How in the world could that do anything but dampen your impact? Isn't the idea of a visual aid to enhance what you're saying?

## Free yourself of the presentation straightjacket

There's another great reason not to put tons of text on your slides. Not only are these slides a horrible distraction for our audience, they put you in a presentation straightjacket, metaphorically speaking. Unless you have "escape artist" in your skill set, this is absolutely as imprisoning as it sounds. Here's why.

Most presenters who suffer from information overloading on their slides utter the same mantra, *"This is really important stuff."* Let's assume for a minute that it is really important stuff.

First of all, putting it on a slide for the audience to read does NOTHING to guarantee they will "get" it, and second, too much of this "really important stuff" puts you in the metaphorical straight jacket. You feel compelled to talk about it because it's up there on the big screen.

You lose the ability to speak off the cuff, respond to a question, tie in to a current event. You don't have time for any of that! You've got too much *really important stuff* to get through. You get bogged down, you find yourself reading what's on the screen — even though you know doing so is a cardinal sin in presentations — because you have no alternative. You MUST address it ALL. About a third of the way through, you find yourself wishing the presentation were over. No such luck, you still have slide after slide PACKED with *really important stuff.*

## A teaser for them = freedom for you

Instead of putting yourself in a straightjacket, how about creating slides that illustrate a few key ideas? Maybe three words, a graph, chart, photo, or diagram? A provocative question or quote? With less stuff of any kind (really important or not), you will be free to go into as much or as little detail as you like. Maybe for one presentation your second point requires expounding, while for another group it's point number three that needs more explanation. The sparseness of your slides enables you to adjust your presentation to your audience, your time frame, your setting, and your own sense of what's more and less important given those three variables. With visuals that elicit your key ideas rather than you having to explain each of them in gory, grueling detail, you create a dynamic, fluid experience for you and your audience. When has anybody ever remembered all the really important stuff spelled out on PowerPoint slides, anyway? (Uh, never.)

Nail It.

---

**An Example from Our PowerPoint Guru:
Nicholas Oulton**

Nick Oulton, owner of M62 Visual Communications and a true PowerPoint guru, has done his own experiment for years regarding PowerPoint slides and audience retention. During his presentation, he shows his audience two slides: one with a list of bullet points and another with a very simple diagram that illustrates those same points. Next, he "fakes" a computer malfunction and asks the audience to recreate the two slides he's just shown on a piece of blank paper. Which slide do you think they can recreate? Yes, it's the diagram. Most can regurgitate only two of the five bullet points from the text-intensive slide. But here's where it gets even more interesting. Not only can Nick's audience recreate the illustration, they can repeat what he talked about while showing the illustration. The audience truly "got it" and got it all when Nick combined a visual with the "Huh?" factor and his oral content. Slam dunk.

---

## See for Yourself: Blah Blah Blah vs True Visual Aid

I use a similar tactic myself, without the "fake-out." First, I show the audience the following slide:

### GREAT POWERPOINT
PRESENTATIONS

- Should never be self-explanatory
- Should never be read aloud by the speaker
- Should always be a synergistic component
- Should always illuminate in ways speaker cannot

I tell them that everything the slide says is accurate, but that as a visual aid the slide is completely ineffective. Then I show the next slide:

This slide says everything the previous slide said but is completely effective as a visual aid. First, it's got the "Huh?" factor. We look at this slide and we think, "Huh?" (Even those of us who never got beyond first-grade math know that one plus one does not equal three.) The audience must look to the presenter (me) to explain what they're looking at and what it means. Second, the simplicity of this slide allows me to talk about it as long as I'd like. If I'm running short on time, or this audience doesn't use a ton of PowerPoint, I'll spend only a minute or two on it. If I have more time, or I know this particular audience uses (and misuses) PowerPoint a lot, I will go into this in more detail. Third, and this took me a while to realize, this slide is "sticky." Not only does it drive the point home, it's got staying power. Months and months after audiences see this slide, they remember it and, more important, remember its message.

I realize that coming up with slides like this requires a certain amount of creativity. Simply putting your notes on slides is way,

way easier. Unfortunately, slides with your notes on them do nothing to aid your audience in getting your message, let alone retaining it. In fact, the more words you put on your slides, the less your audience will retain. When it comes to visuals, less is always more. (This is a mantra that works for presentations in general.)

# Essentials for Visuals

### ONE big idea per slide

The number of slides you have in your presentation is not an issue; what is on them is. For example, you could have a ten-slide deck with twelve bullets of paragraphs on each slide. Yuck. Conversely, you could have a thirty-slide deck with one phrase on each slide, or some slides with one to three short phrases, some slides with diagrams, and a few with charts or graphs. Now those would be good, helpful visual aids!

### Visibility a MUST

First, and most important, every visual you create must be able to be seen from anywhere in the audience. There is nothing worse than a slide going up on a screen and hearing the presenter say, "You can't really see this but . . . " Seriously?? If it cannot be seen by everyone, do not show it.

### Make it easy for the audience

Second, all text should be vertical so that it can easily be read left to right. This applies to vertical-axis labels as well. I hate seeing audience members turning their (heavy) heads perpendicular to their necks trying to read the $Y$ axis.

## No fancy fonts

Use only sans-serif fonts for all text: Arial, Calibri, Tahoma, and Verdana are examples of sans-serif fonts. (This means the boring-looking fonts without short lines adorning the letter strokes.) I advise against anything "artsy" — no shadows, italics, or florescent colors. This is not the time or place to get creative. The idea is for the audience to read the FEW words you have on the screen easily and immediately bring their attention back to you.

## Small is not beautiful

No text type size should be smaller than twenty-points. This may come as a huge shock to some of you whose slides look more like the white pages of the phone book than they do billboards. Remember, words aren't great visual aids anyway. Less is more, and readability is critical.

## Brand!

Use your company's colors. Any presentation you give should be an extension of your brand. It should remind the audience of who you are, what you're about, and what value you bring. That's all tied up in your brand, represented by your logo and its colors.

## Simpler is always better

It's all I can do not to bust out laughing when a new client says to me, "Make it do all the fancy stuff. You know, I want the words to fly in, bounce in, checkerboard in. And let's have a bunch of those cute clip-art things that move back and forth. And some great photos, too. And I like different fonts . . . stuff like that." Aye yai yai. If the most memorable thing about your presentation is the way the material appears on the screen, you've got BIG problems.

Nail It.

## Be a control freak

If you use bullets, flow charts, or bar charts, make them build. Animate them so that the audience sees one piece of the chart at a time or one bullet at a time. As the presenter, you want to control the flow of information. It's best to feed it to the audience one bite at a time. If you don't, they'll gulp it all down at once or will be looking at different parts of the slide and become increasingly lost and confused.

For example, if you put up a slide with five bullets, they'll quickly read all five while you're talking about bullet number one. They'll then tune in to you, only to hear you talking about, well, they're not sure what you're talking about since they weren't paying attention while they were reading. Now they're lost so they figure they'll just surf their Blackberries or iPhones until the next slide comes up (and curse you for not simply emailing them the presentation so they could read it snuggled up at home in their pj's.)

## Make transitions invisible

This will allow the audience to focus their full attention on you. The animations should be what PowerPoint describes as subtle. They appear, fade, or wipe. Once you choose an animation method for a slide deck, all slides in the deck should animate in the same

### When You Want Their Focus Solely on the Screen (courtesy of Nick Oulton)

If you are showing a video clip, a quote, or something else that requires the audience's complete attention, turn your back to the audience and look at the screen yourself. This lets them know unequivocally where their focus should be. Once the clip is finished, turn back toward them. When their eyes meet yours, you can move on.

way. In fact, everything about the way the visuals come onto the screen should be invisible to the audience — unless you're rolling out a new product or huge initiative, and then maybe you'll have a BIG GIANT slide to announce it.

## When It's Time for Questions

When taking questions, either have a slide that says simply, "Questions ?" or a blank screen. (Another tip from Nick Oulton.) Touching the *B* key on the keyboard will blacken the screen, and touching *B* again will bring it back. The *W* key will white the screen. I prefer the *B* key because it's easier on the audience's eyes. DO NOT leave anything up on the screen (text, a chart, or graph) that will distract them. Despite the fact that they've already read it, the audience will read any text left on the screen over and over and over . . .

At the conclusion of the presentation, simply put your logo, or your logo with contact information, up on the screen.

## Delivery and PowerPoint Slides

No matter what kind of slides or other visuals you're using, the following guidelines are worth keeping in mind.

First, YOU are the most important visual of your presentation, not your slides. You are and should be the focus. The visuals are there to enhance your message, not to upstage you. With that in mind, please, please keep your focus on your audience and NOT on the screen. If you are showing a chart or graph, you may have to look at it to explain the axis, the trend, or whatever. But once you do that, you must return your focus to your audience. Too much time spent looking at your slides diminishes your connection to your audience. Not good.

Second (I know I'm repeating here; it's intentional), DO NOT read what's on the slide, even if it is only three words. Rephrase them, expound on them, talk around or about them, or weave them into a complete sentence. Two or three words are easy for an audience to read and still maintain focus on you. They've already read the words — and faster than you can read them aloud. Refraining from reading them with the audience helps make your presentation more dynamic.

Third, there is absolutely no reason to say things like, "This slide talks about . . ." (slides don't talk!) or even "This next slide . . ." In fact, try not to say the word *slide* at all. Instead, while they're looking at a line graph, say something like, "When we look at the history of the past ten years of plastics sales, we see that . . . "

## Think outside the Screen

Not every visual aid needs to be a PowerPoint slide, nor does it need to be something on a flip chart, foam board, or white board. Step outside the world of the one dimensional and think 3–D. Can you think of a prop you could use to illustrate your point?

I use six bouncy balls (big ones) to drive home my plea to keep one's main points to no more than five in any presentation. (You can go to www.bespeakpresentations.com, and click on the Presentations and Props video to see this.) Unfailingly, when I see someone who has seen my presentation, they will introduce me as, "the lady with the balls." Okay, so that may not be the world's most desirable nickname, but they remember the idea behind the balls. Sticky sticky sticky. It's a visual that's a hit. (Plus, it's got the "Huh?" factor and can be seen from anywhere in the room.)

A client of mine who gives small group presentations about bio-identical hormone replacement therapy thought of using Tinker Toys to show the molecular structure of a hormone and how it's altered by pharmaceutical companies in order to be patented. Not only is this a great 3–D visual, it drives the point home in ways she alone cannot.

Think about your presentation and its main points. Are there 3–D things you can use as visuals rather than a slide or flip chart? Using this kind of unusual aid will not only help your audience get your message, it will also set you apart from and above other presenters. More important, it will increase the odds they'll remember you, your presentation, and — most important of all — your ideas long after it's over.

## Handouts

Whenever adults, or anyone old enough to read, are given reading material, they will happily, immediately put their heads down and begin reading. Because of this, you should NEVER give an audience a text-intensive handout until you've finished speaking. If you see them rushing to take notes, you can reassure them that you've got the contents on a handout, which you'll be giving out at the conclusion of the presentation.

When giving informative or educational presentations, it's helpful to give out a bare-bones outline with big spaces for note taking. This can absolutely be given out before you begin speaking, as it serves as a tool to help your audience jot down important information. For persuasive presentations, you want the audience's full attention. They should not be preoccupied with extensive note taking. In fact, leave-behinds with the five benefits of your product, service, or proposal are great as reinforcers. Again, these should be given only at the conclusion.

Nail It.

## Take Aways

- Use your visuals as synergistic partners.

- Team up with them and together make your message clear and unforgettable.

- Make sure they truly aid the audience in understanding your ideas.

- They should be big, bold, and brief and visible from anywhere in the room.

- They should have the "Huh?" factor. Your audience should look at the visual and then immediately look to you for explanation.

- Never give an audience anything to read until you are finished speaking.

- And remember, YOU are your greatest visual. The other stuff is simply aiding you.

# 4
# The Presenter

At last, we get to the component about which you, the reader, are most interested: YOURSELF. (Readers are a lot like audience members. Kind of makes you think all of us are going through life tuned in to the WIIFM [What's in it for me?] channel, doesn't it?) Now that you've assessed your audience, built your presentation specifically with them in mind, and created accompanying visuals that will truly aid you in getting your message across, you're ready for your big moment. Right? Well, almost. Here are some important guidelines, tips, and tools to ensure all your hard work will pay off.

## Be YOU

The most important thing you can do to connect with your audience is to be YOURSELF. No kidding. You don't have to be beautiful, funny, or even charismatic. If you happen to be any of those things, congratulations! Use your gifts wisely. The rest of us will have to be content with just being ourselves. Frankly, being you is the most important thing you can be, and here's why.

Whenever you meet someone for the first time, the first thing you're determining, immediately and virtually unconsciously, is your level of trust. If the person you're meeting makes eye contact, smiles warmly, even shyly, and feels authentic and sincere, you allow yourself to trust him or her, albeit provisionally at first. The longer you are in contact with this person and the more consistent his or her behavior, the more trust develops. Conversely, if you meet someone who doesn't make eye contact, doesn't smile, doesn't feel authentic or sincere, your guard immediately goes up. You will be skeptical and untrusting of that individual. What's more, it will take a lot of time and effort on his or her part to negate your first impression.

What occurs when watching a presenter is that same dynamic you experience in a one-on-one meeting. Your first concern, before subject matter, length of speech, and even viewpoint, is trustworthiness. Bert Decker, a longtime presentation expert, talks about this human phenomenon in his book *You've Got To Be Believed To Be Heard* (2008). He says it goes all the way back to our beginnings on the planet.

## Are you for real?

Whatever its origin, in plain language the audience wants to know "Are you for real?" "Do YOU believe what you're saying?" "Are you willing to let us in?" "Do you really care about us?" If the answers to these questions are affirmative, they will let you in. They will trust you. They will LISTEN.

Therefore, it is absolutely imperative that you BE YOURSELF. Trust your audience to accept you for you, unfunny, overweight, bald. Who cares? You're not asking them to be you, you're asking them to listen to you. One-of-a-kind, sincere, authentic, 100% YOU. Once they see that you're the real deal, then and only then will they be open to what it is you have to say.

As easy as this is to do, or maybe because it's so easy to do, I get push-back on it all the time. For example, clients come to me and say, "I need you to make me funny." This is a bad news/good news scenario. The bad news is, I can't make anybody funny. If I try to put words in your mouth that get a HUGE laugh when I say them, you could deliver the same line and the result would be "crickets," as my elder daughter would say. (The room would be so quiet you could hear crickets.) Conversely, you could say something that gets an audience to ROAR with laughter, but it would not get the same reaction were I to say it.

The good news is this: you don't have to be funny in order to be effective. If you think back to your favorite teachers and professors, you would maybe remember two out of five who were funny. What they were was real. They were sincere. They had enthusiasm for and knowledge of their subject. Funny? Who cared? And while we're at it, they probably weren't the best looking, best dressed, hippest, or even nicest. What they were was totally, unequivocally authentic.

In fact, I would offer that authenticity is in itself charismatic. Many of us are afraid to let our own light really shine, yet we gravitate toward and celebrate those who do. Ironically, we don't recognize that they are, in fact, just being themselves. We think we need to be like them in order to be successful, to be liked, to be heard.

Nothing could be more wrong. What you need to do is turn up the volume on your own authenticity and uniqueness. That is the only way to draw people toward you.

Oscar Wilde said, "Be yourself. Everyone else is already taken." My mom says, "Celebrate your differentness." I say, "Be you. Be heard."

## Be You: Breaking It Down

When I say "be you," I mean it. This means that some of the "rules" you learned about good public speaking may have to go out the window. Trust me and try it my way. Years of working with different kinds of people of all ages, backgrounds, and professions has convinced me that being oneself is critical to being heard.

---

### Celebrate Your "Differentness"

When I was a child we moved just about every year. Being the "new kid" was stressful enough when the move was relatively local, but moving to various parts of the country meant I always arrived in the new place with a "weird accent." Some of the words for things differed in different parts of the country as well. "Soda" in Pittsburg was "pop" in Detroit. In addition to external differences, I was tiny for my age, wore glasses, was kind of funny looking and talked incessantly. Even if we'd lived in the same place forever, I'd have been raising eyebrows.

My mother's advice? "Celebrate your differentness." She wouldn't hear my complaining that I didn't sound like the other kids, or talk like the other kids, or look or even act like the other kids. She was determined to convince me that true happiness lay in celebrating who I was. Size 13 baby shoe and all. It is good, solid, happy-making advice in life and in public speaking. Those of us who can truly celebrate who we are are happier for it. We are standing on more solid ground than our unsure, insecure counterparts. And we draw people to us.

---

## "What do I do with my hands?"

Here's a question I get over and over. The answer is "DO you." If you talk with your hands (and some of us can't talk without them), you should absolutely talk with your hands when presenting. Use your hands as you would when in an animated conversation with a friend. Make sure you use your hands purposefully, and not as a way to expend nervous energy. When speaking to larger groups, when it comes to gestures, the bigger the better.

If you are more sedate in conversation and you rarely gesture, then a presentation is not the time to start. To try using your hands when it is not comfortable will look awkward and disingenuous.

No matter what is coming out of your mouth, the audience will sense the incongruity. They may not be able to put their finger on it, but it will bother them just the same. More important, you will be focusing on this new and unnatural movement instead of focusing on your audience and your subject matter. This is a bad use of your energy, and certainly not a way to induce comfort.

In the 2008 election, John McCain made the mistake of trying to gesture in ways that were unnatural to him. (His speech writers didn't help him, either. His speeches were reading material, not speech-worthy material.) He consistently looked wooden, awkward, fake. Subconsciously we wondered, how could this "maverick" look so uncomfortable in his own skin? He was unable to truly be himself, and consequently, the American people didn't find it easy to connect with him.

## Hey, Man. What's up with the Arm Lock?

A few years ago I had the honor of coaching a management consultant from one of the top companies in that industry. This gentleman was an excellent speaker — articulate, enthusiastic, knowledgeable. Unfortunately, he'd received some bad advice from a semi-famous speaking coach in New York City. Here was my client, effusively speaking, with his right hand in a death grip on his left arm. His arms, restricted by each other, were flapping up and down like wings desperately trying to take the poor man into flight. When I politely inquired, "What's the deal with your arms locked up like that?" he informed me that his semi-famous trainer had told him NOT to move his hands, only his feet. Huh? Once he agreed to try setting his arms free (and with them, his hands), he was able to gesture naturally and effectively. His entire presentation came together, and his message came through loud and clear.

Nail It.

## The MYTH of the 7%–38%–55% Principle

Chances are you've heard some well-meaning public speaking "expert" tell you that only 7% of what an audience takes away from your presentation is in the content, 38% is voice, and 55% is body language and gestures. You may have immediately panicked because you're not much of a gesture-er, not big on modulating your voice, just really focused on your content. Well, breathe a big sigh of relief because these statistics have been misrepresented for decades. The author of the study that produced the statistics, Albert Mehrabian, researched a listener's divining of a speaker's true feelings behind his or her message. In other words, if I say, "I love my mother" and I put both hands over my heart and get a little choked up, you, the listener, absolutely believe that I do, in fact, love my mother. My message is in alignment with my tone and gestures. If I say, "I love my mother" while rolling my eyes and accentuating the word *love,* you hear and see the sarcasm in my voice and movements and believe the opposite: I'm not so crazy about my mother. My vocal tone and gestures far outweigh my words. THIS, my dear presenter, was the conclusion of Mehrabian's research. It was all about the speaker's feelings about what he or she was saying. Mehrabian, in his book *Silent Messages,* made explicit that "we should be careful to note that these assertions about the disproportionate contribution of implicit, relative to verbal, cues is limited to feelings and like–dislike."

What does this mean for you, the presenter? Simply that your facial expressions, your gestures (or lack thereof), and your vocal inflection must match your message. If you don't believe what you're saying, the audience will know it. More important, if your gestures are not your own (as in, *choreographed* for you), your message will ring false. The audience may not know why, but they'll know that something is not syncing. It does not mean that you should be wildly gesticulating or modulating your vocal tone artificially. This will only scream PHONY, not — as some would have you believe — powerful.

While innate movement is key, do not allow yourself to sway back and forth, or wring your hands, or play with a pen because "that's you." That's not you, that's your nervous energy. That kind of movement is distracting and must be avoided. Purposeful gesturing, if that is your natural style, is excellent and should be exploited. On the other hand, those of you who speak without using your hands can be equally effective.

## Accents

Unless your accent is so thick that it will prohibit your audience from understanding you, there is no need to worry about it or try to eliminate it. I promise you that once your audience becomes accustomed to it, they will forget about it and focus on your message. If you are really self-conscious about it, you can make some kind of self-deprecating comment at the outset. "Believe it or not, I spent the first twelve years of my life in Peru. If you listen closely, you may be able to hear my accent." This kind of statement puts everyone at ease. If you do have a strong accent, it is necessary to speak slowly and articulate well. If your accent is so strong that you know you won't be easily understood, look for a communication coach who specializes in minimizing accents. Here on the East Coast, my colleague Vicki Mackenzie specializes in helping folks diminish their accents.

## Voice

If you are soft-spoken, or speak in a monotone, that's okay, too. Audiences are endlessly forgiving about this kind of thing as long as the message you convey has meaning for them. In fact, your soft voice or monotone helps your message to take center stage in a more undistracted way. A softer voice will also force an audience to quiet themselves and listen more closely.

Nail It.

Be very careful, however, never to talk so softly that they have to strain to hear you. Nothing will make an audience madder faster than not being able to hear a speaker. If you hear mumbling in the audience and you know yourself to be soft-spoken, be sure to ask, "Can everyone hear me?" If they respond with "No," you MUST speak louder.

---

## Take Aways

- You must be yourself in order for your audience to be able to connect with you.

- Do whatever you normally do with your hands when in animated conversation with a friend or family member. DO NOT choreograph your presentation with other people's gestures.

- Be genuine. If you don't believe what you're saying, your audience will know it.

- Don't worry about an accent unless it is very, very strong.

- Celebrate your "differentness"; your willingness to share your true self will attract the audience to you.

## Ursula the Sea Witch as Real Estate Speculator

Years ago I was invited to attend a presentation for real estate investors. A builder and a realtor had joined forces to build a property with the help of investors in the hopes of selling it for a hefty profit. The presentation was informal, taking place on a Sunday afternoon. A junior member of the real estate arm turned the "stage" over to the builder. Lo and behold, a woman about six feet tall, in her mid- to late sixties, stood and began, "Don't mind the cough. It's pneumonia, but it's not contagious."

Her physical appearance was diametrically opposed to the ideas of "promotion" and "construction." She had one of the sorrier body shapes I'd ever seen, protruding where a woman's body typically inverts and vice versa. The snug black knit outfit she had on only emphasized her figure. In addition, her slip was flying like a flag outside the slit of her skirt. Her hair was a blonde not known in the natural hair color spectrum; her make-up was both too pale (skin) and too bright (lips and eyes). In addition, she was sporting an inordinate amount of jewelry, both cosmetic and real, all of which looked expensive, none of which matched itself or her outfit.

But once she began talking about real estate investment in general and the property she was designing and building in particular, all thoughts and preoccupations about her appearance drifted away.

This woman was the real deal. Her explanations of how profit was to be gained through this investment were presented in such a solid, understandable way that a six-year-old would have understood her. Her reasoning and enthusiasm for her project were infectious. Despite an uncanny resemblance to Ursula the Sea Witch from Disney's "The Little Mermaid," she was one of the best presenters I'd ever seen. Was the audience momentarily distracted by her appearance, her attire, and her really scary cough? Sure. But once she started her presentation, all that went away. She had us eating out of her (possibly germ-riddled) hand.

The moral of the story? Focus on your message and its relevance to your audience. That's where their focus will be.

# Be Quiet

Okay, I know this sounds antithetical to public speaking. How can you speak and be quiet? I'm talking about the non-verbal and verbal things we have a tendency to do that speak so loudly, they prevent our audience from hearing our message.

Keep in mind that frequency is a key factor in determining whether a behavior is really distracting your audience. The occasional shuffle of the feet, hands through the hair, or "um" or "ah" will not pose a problem. Constant shuffling of feet, hands through the hair, and so on will be so loud your message won't be heard.

### Third Time's a Charm

A word about video and you. Anytime you watch yourself on tape, you must watch it at least three times. Why? The first time we watch ourselves on film we react to the way we look, and usually negatively. "My hair looks like that?" or "I've gotta go on a diet!" are typical reactions to first viewings.

The second viewing is even worse. This time we're picking apart every little thing we did wrong. We're the president of the "I hate me" fan club. We watch with self-loathing, vowing never to set foot in front of an audience again, possibly even outside our own homes or bedrooms. You get the idea.

Finally, the third time we watch ourselves on video it is with a more objective eye. We can even see some things we did right! We hear good arguments we made, realize how great we look when we smile, hear the audience laugh at something funny we said. "Hey," we think, "maybe I'm not so bad after all. Maybe I should accept that next opportunity to speak." (Well, after we get our hair cut and lose a few pounds . . .)

The best way to determine whether you are guilty of this unproductive "noise" is either to film yourself giving a presentation or have a trusted friend, who loves you no matter what, watch you present and let you know whether you're "noisy."

## Non-Verbal Distractors

Physical distractors are damaging to your audience's focus. Often, we're simply repeating some physical action because it releases pent up energy and nerves. While I am a big fan of purposeful movement, nervous energy movement is its polar opposite. Movement should be motivated by either your message or your audience. What follows are just some of the more common examples of non-verbal noise. Lord knows you've probably been witness to or the victim of many more. Remember, awareness is the first step toward change.

### Playing with your clothes

I'll start with men, but women are equally guilty of clothes-play. Men have an unfortunate tendency to pull their sport coat or suit coat lapels together when they stand up to present, and often will keep pulling it together. (This may be why some presentation trainers suggest that men should button their coats when they stand to speak.) I think the problem may be that when the presenter bought the sport coat he wore a size 42, and now he wears a size 44 . . . Pulling at the sides of the jacket won't make it bigger, nor will it make you slimmer. You have to give in and buy a bigger jacket. Whatever you're wearing should fit comfortably and look terrific, and you should feel terrific wearing it. Which brings me to the ladies.

Women have a tendency to fiddle with their blouses, sweaters, jackets. I can only think they are trying to cover up the chest or stomach area of their bodies. Unfortunately, the more they pull and fiddle with their tops, the more our attention is drawn there. When you fidget with your clothing, you may subconsciously be thinking you're covering up a figure flaw, but in reality you're drawing attention to it and — WORSE — you're distracting your audience! That's a lose-lose. Let me say (which I will, over and over again throughout this book) that your audience really doesn't care at all if you've gained a few pounds or lost your bustline after giving birth. They pretty much don't care about you at all, except as to how what you're saying will benefit them. If you find yourself guilty of this, you must wear clothing that is fiddle-proof. Period.

Wear something you feel great in and forget about it.

## Pen play

We've all had the teacher, professor, or speaker who held a pen or pencil in one hand and made it go up and down up and down up and down. After a while the pen becomes hypnotic. We're not hearing the speaker's message anymore because we've been hypnotized by the pen. Our own heads may even be bobbing up and down along with the pen.

Equally distracting is the Mad Clicker, the speaker who holds the pen in his hand and incessantly clicks its end. After a while all you can hear is the click click click of the pen. It becomes like some awful *Twilight Zone* episode where the pen gets louder and louder and the speaker's mouth is moving, but you can't hear him.

PLEASE, if you know you have a tendency to play with a pen, DON'T hold one. This goes for client meetings, board meetings — anywhere you'll be speaking with or to another person. (Side note: if you're a nervous speaker, you can hold a marker in your hand so that you're gripping it by the body. All your nervous energy can then shoot straight down your arm and into your death grip on the marker — and NO ONE WILL NOTICE. Once you've gotten through the first minute or two of your presentation and you're feeling more confident, you can put the marker down. This will help dissipate nervous energy, and no one will be the wiser.)

## Hand jive

Sometimes rather than moving your feet to expel nervous energy, you repeat a certain hand movement. One of my clients continually moved both her hands in a forward circular motion during her presentation. By itself, this looked like a good gesture. Once we had worked on the content of her presentation, however, and we looked at both the old and new versions on tape, she realized the circular hands in her "old version" were an outcome of insecurity about her material. She hadn't known where she was going next, and her motions were an extension of her nervous energy rather than a physical way of further explaining her message. In the tape of the revised presentation, her hand gestures are purposeful and forceful, enhancing her message.

## Hair play

If you have a tendency to run your hands through your hair when you get nervous, put it back in a ponytail, barrette, head band, or other restraint. Take away the option of playing with it.

## Eyeglasses: Can we talk?

For those of us over (ahem) forty, reading glasses become a necessary evil. PLEASE do not allow them to become a plaything or any other kind of distracter. Either wear them or don't, for starters. If you have to take them on and off, practice doing it so the act is natural and fluid. (I once saw a presenter spend what seemed like minutes searching for her glasses every time she needed them during her presentation. I wanted to stand up and shout: "They're on the podium where you left them!" You can always wear them on a chain around your neck or hold them in your hand. Just don't lose them and have to hunt for them while the audience watches and waits.

Nail It.

## Pockets

I have no problem with presenters putting a hand in a pocket, but, for heaven's sake, take the change and keys out before you stand up to present! Presenters' pockets should be empty. And only one hand in a pants pocket at a time, please. A hand in each pocket for more than a few seconds looks awkward, and as you relax you'll start moving your elbows in a rooster-on-the-lawn kind of way.

More problematic are index cards or papers you may have to hold to refer to during your presentation. If you find yourself fiddling with them, PUT THEM DOWN. Pick them up to refer to, and put them down again. (Just remember where you put them.)

## Dancin' feet

If you're guilty of any kind of purposeless foot movement, you need to put a stop to it. Particularly during your introduction, it is important that you stand still so your audience can get a good, clear look at you.

If you are presenting to a large group, moving from one side of the stage or one part of the room to another is a great way to connect with your audience. Move across the stage or the room confidently and with intention; then stand still. No pacing back and forth across the stage. I refer to this as the cougar-in-the-cage move. It's great for comedians who are dishing out tiny bites of communication, but not so good for presenters who are stringing together ideas. Comedians can do it. You can't.

I once witnessed a man give a seven-minute extemporaneous speech at a Toastmaster's meeting. The entire time he spoke he was moving his feet to a dance step that was either the samba, the rumba, or the cha cha. I've never taken dance lessons, but I swear it was one of those three. Talk about distracting. I have no idea what the substance of his speech was, but boy was I mesmerized by his dancin' feet.

If you're a foot shuffler, pacer, or samba dancer, stand still! Imagine you are standing atop a pillar. Plant your weight on the balls of your feet. Stay still until you're comfortable there, and then you can experiment with moving out from the point of a *V* and then back to center. Practice your speech at home with particular cues to moves. Maybe just after your introduction you'll move to the left segment of the audience, and then after you've made your first supporting point, you'll move back to center.

## Eliminating Non-Verbal Distractors

The very best way to eliminate any non-verbal audience distractor is first to be made aware of it. Filming yourself in action and watching the film is by far the best way to accomplish this. If film isn't possible, have a trusted friend act as your eyes and ears. Remember, do NOT let anyone suggest gestures for you. Use your hands as you would in extra-animated conversation with a friend. Wear clothes you feel covered, comfortable, and confident in, and most important: Be YOU.

## Verbal Audience Distractors

### *Um*'s and *ah*'s

First of all, understand that *um*'s and *ah*'s and other non-words come from a little brain hiccup, nerves, and a fear of unfilled space. We're terrified about what will happen if sound stops coming out of our mouths for three seconds. Do you know what happens when sound stops coming out of your mouth for three seconds? You get the audience's attention. Empty space is good. Really good. In fact, pauses can be as, if not more, powerful than words. They can signify to the audience that you've said something so important that you want them to take a minute to let it sink in.

Typically you um and ah if you're simply pausing to gather your thoughts, which takes way less than three seconds. Allow silence rather than filling the space with a non-word. *Um*'s and *ah*'s require listening and filtering. Instead, take a breath and give your listeners the opportunity to gather their thoughts. They are working hard to process the information you're providing. A brief silence allows them time to organize mentally and regroup. This is a huge gift. By the way, it's a huge gift to you as well. The silence will make it much easier for you to stop, think, and move on to your next point.

Lastly, allowing a brief silence tells your audience that you are comfortable with standing quietly in front of them. It communicates power and control, the demeanor of a real pro. (Yes, you.)

### *You know*'s and *I mean*'s

*You know*'s and *I mean*'s come from a different place then *um*'s and *ah*'s. While *um*'s and *ah*'s are place-fillers, *you know*'s and *I mean*'s are a subconscious sign that you're unsure about your message. "You know" is asking for the audience's buy-in, approval, or agreement. "I mean" is your way of restating and re-sorting. Neither of these is helpful in conversation. They distract and diminish the power of your presentation. You do not want to be asking the audience, over and over, to agree with you, nor do you want to ask for their patience while you rephrase and rephrase.

Worse, *you know*'s and *I mean*'s, unlike *um*'s and *ah*'s, are real words! The audience hears these as plausible parts of your presentation and then must weed them out. Whew! That's a lot of work to ask of someone. It's exhausting. So exhausting that some in the audience may opt to simply tune out the presenter rather than continue with the grueling task of deconstructing and reassembling his or her message.

## Eliminating Verbal Distractors

Thus, you must eliminate these two verbal distractors from your speech as well. How to accomplish this? It's actually quite easy. First, you need to become aware of what's coming out of your mouth. You may think you are, but I can pretty much guarantee you aren't. At least, not when you're speaking in front of people and other things are demanding your attention: their responses, where you're headed next, and so on. I recommend eliminating words (*you know*'s and *I mean*'s) or non-words (*um*'s and *ah*'s) well before your next presentation. Start with normal, day-to-day conversations so that you're accustomed to the process before you set foot in front of an audience.

Begin by directing your focus 35° inward, not 90°, which would prevent you from being attentive to whomever you're communicating with. Think of rearview mirrors turned in so that you can see inside your car — in this case, yourself. Perfect. Now start talking. Uh-oh, here's where the frustrating part is. You'll catch yourself *um*'ing and *ah*'ing, you *know*'ing and I *mean*'ing, but not until the sounds or words have escaped your mouth. I'm warning you, it's a little crazy-making, but stick with it. In a matter of hours you'll begin to stop these words and non-words before they get to your mouth. You'll allow a beat of blissful silence to take their place. Bravo! Well done, you! Now the trick is simply to turn this focus "on" whenever you stand up to speak.

## Give yourself twenty-one days . . .

Being silent rather than using words or non-words as placeholders or insecurity fillers may feel unnatural at first, but keep at it. (Remember, it takes twenty-one days to make a new habit or eliminate one.) You've probably been *um*'ing or *ah*'ing or you *know*'ing and I *mean*'ing for years; it will take a little while to unlearn. But remember, although the silence of a pause feels awkward to you, to your audience it's a gift. And don't worry about a big span of unfilled space. It truly is just a millisecond.

Remember, silence is golden. And powerful. And even more important, not distracting. Don't try to fill empty spaces with non-words. Stop asking your audience for reinforcement and approval with *you know*'s and *I mean*'s. Instead, give them the gift of silence.

### Time Stands Still — or Does It?

Years ago I was in a play in which I had a twelve-minute monologue. I had practiced for weeks and knew it inside out and backward, when one night in the middle of a performance, my mind went "black." I mean black. Nothing was there. I don't think I could have told you my name. I stood there on stage, alone, nodding and smiling at the audience, mind black as night. It felt like an eighteen-car train could have been run through that silence. I was almost ready to turn and walk off the stage when, mercifully, the lines came back to me and I continued on. As luck would have it, the show was taped that night. I was eager (and terrified) to see my huge gaff. Unbelievably, when I watched the tape I couldn't find the spot where I'd gone blank. I replayed the monologue several times. Where was the vastness I had felt as I stood there praying to be beamed off the stage? As it turned out, what had felt like a lifetime to me was actually not even ten seconds in real-world time. No one in the audience could have known.

## Rapid-fire speech

If you have a tendency to talk faster than the speed of light, I hope someone has alerted you to this by now. If, however, you speak rapidly only when you are nervous, you may not be aware of this behavior. Often when we know our material cold we forget that for the audience this is all new stuff. When speaking, make sure you sustain eye contact with different individuals in the audience long enough to determine whether they understand your message. This will both slow you down (because your mind will be forced to multi-task) and let you know from their facial expressions whether they are working too hard to follow you. By the way, it never hurts to ask, "Am I going too fast?" It's a great way to get your audience involved and let them know you really care about them. And if you are going too fast, they'll tell you.

## Take Aways

- If you see yourself doing one or more of these audience distracters, don't despair. Awareness is the first step toward change.

- If you're a pen clicker, DON'T hold the pen.

- If you've a tendency to fiddle with your clothes, buy a bigger sport coat or wear something that doesn't allow for pulling.

- If you're a paper or note card shredder, write your bullets on index cards and then laminate them so they're unshreddable.

- Eliminate the object of your distracting behavior. Whatever the object, it can be either eliminated or changed to prevent you from creating a distraction for your audience.

- Move with purpose, ideally as transitions in your message occur. Remember, when you stand still, straight, and tall you can feel your own power rising from your feet to the tip of your head. It is this power, plus the power of your message, that gives you strength and compels your audience to listen.

- If you pepper sentences with *um*'s or *ah*'s, *you know*'s or *I mean*'s, begin today to really think while you're speaking. Catch yourself emitting non-words in the beginning, middle, or end of a thought. Consciously prohibit yourself from making those sounds. Remember, they're distracting your own thought process as well. YOU can listen to yourself more easily without all those non-words in the way.

You want your audience to listen to your message. Let's make that easy for them. Limit the verbal and non-verbal distracters that keep your message from being heard.

# Be Connecting

If you are a nervous or reticent speaker, chances are someone along the way advised you to "just look over the audiences' heads." While that may possibly make you less nervous, it will not help your message be heard.

Why must you actually make eye contact with your audience? Because that's your way to connect with them, and you must connect in order to deliver your message. "The eyes are the windows to the soul" some wise person said. In order to truly communicate with you, I must be looking at you. If I'm not looking at you, how do I know if you understand what I'm saying? How do I know if I'm losing you, whether you agree or disagree, whether you're tired, bored, enthused, enjoying yourself? I can gather this information only by looking directly at you.

Think about the last time you were part of an audience. Didn't you want to make eye contact with the speaker? Almost subconsciously, you want to connect with the speaker. You want him to connect with you. It drives the message home for you when you feel the speaker has looked you in the eye and spoken to you directly. Right?

## Don't scare 'em away

This does not mean, however, that you should punish the good listener by speaking (and looking) only at him or her. Perhaps you've had the hugely uncomfortable experience of being a good, active listener and suddenly feeling as though you were the only person in the room. The speaker is looking directly at you for what seems like an eternity. You feel yourself blushing, sweating. You look away. Now you're afraid to make eye contact with the presenter again for fear she'll lock in on you and suck your soul out through your eyes. You look down, praying for her presentation to be over.

Sound familiar? Don't be guilty of focusing only on one or two audience members. Use the three-second rule when presenting. Look at an audience member for about three seconds before moving on. I find myself dividing up thoughts in threes. I'll look at one person for the beginning, another in the middle, and finish with a third. Whatever works for you, as long as you're making eye contact with different members of the entire audience in short segments.

## Get up close and personal

Don't be afraid to go out into the audience and get within touching distance. This is thrilling for them. You're the speaker, the focus. As you get closer, their heart rates elevate. They become more engaged. "She's coming toward me!" their eternally youthful minds are saying.

Moving among your audience members tells them that you consider yourself one with them, that you're not afraid of them. In fact, you're eager to get closer. This is exciting for them as well as heart-warming.

Another great way to connect with your audience is to call out members by name. "John and I were chatting before the presentation and he told me . . ." This has several benefits: John feels appreciated and honored to be mentioned, and the general audience is impressed you know some of their names and you've had real interaction with some of them. This tells them you're sincerely interested in them. You've proved this by making connections with some of them. All happy-making stuff.

Referring to real scenarios in their lives or businesses is a great way to connect as well. Nothing is more off-putting to an audience than hearing a presenter give an example that has no relevance to them. You can hear the mumbling and see the arms crossing in front of the chests. "He doesn't get us," and "That doesn't happen here," are the thought bubbles over everyone's heads. Make sure you're using examples from their experience. Then the thought bubbles will be, "Hey, this guy gets us!" That will take you miles and miles.

## Connect before "showtime"

For those of you who are fearful speakers, take this next piece of advice to heart.

Before you begin your presentation, make a point of meeting and speaking briefly with a few or your audience members. Here's why. We all love knowing celebrities, and believe it or not, as the speaker, that's you. If you take the time to meet and get to know a few members of the audience, you will have created your own fan club. When you stand up to speak they'll be smiling, nodding, silently cheering you on. They'll turn to the person sitting next to them and whisper, "I got to talk to him before this started. He's really nice. Maybe I can introduce you after this is over." You may think I'm being funny here, but I'm not kidding.

Now when you stand up to speak you'll be looking out into an audience of friends, people rooting for your success. What could be better than that? How about this: You refer to them and something you learned from them that relates to your message. NOW you've got everyone's attention. They see that you've truly connected with another audience member and are making them famous by referring to them in your speech! In addition, they can relate to your example and thus become more eager to hear what you have to say. Now you've got 'em eating out of your hand.

## Take Aways

- Look your audience members in the eyes! That's the only way you can truly connect with them.

- Have three-second "conversations" with each person. Don't sustain eye contact for too much longer than that or it will feel awkward to them.

- If you can, move close to them, even among them.

- Call audience members by name.

- Refer to their lives, their businesses, their experiences.

- Meet and greet them before the presentation begins. They'll be your instant fan club.

# Presentation Etiquette

Whether you're speaking to a large or a small audience, in a boardroom or a banquet hall, these guidelines will keep you on your best footing. As my mother-in-law always said, "Pretty is as pretty does."

## Attire

Always dress one level of formality greater than your audience. If they're in "business casual," wear a suit or something similar, something you'd wear to an interview. If they're in casual attire (for golfing, sight-seeing), you should be in business casual. This means a sport coat for men, slacks, skirt and a sweater or blouse for women. For any speaking engagement, women presenters should wear nothing low-cut or revealing and nothing too short. No high, high heels or big jewelry. I hope it goes without saying that clothes should fit properly, be unwrinkled, clean, and in good repair. If you've worn casual shoes to get to the site (sneakers, snow boots) make sure you change into your presentation shoes before you get there. Under no circumstances should you be changing any article of clothing where anyone can see you.

## Gadgets

Only electronic devices critical to the presentation should be visible (or audible). Cell phones, laptops, and tablets should be turned off and out of sight unless they're being used in the presentation. Remember, you want to eliminate audience distractions. Seeing your cell phone or tablet will take attention away from you.

## Remember: You're always ON

From the time you enter the site of the presentation, whether it's a hotel, an office building, or a convention hall, assume you are being watched and evaluated. This is not the time to argue with your teenager or check on your flight or catch up with your office. If the conference or meeting involves a meal, use that opportunity to engage in polite conversation with those around you. Again, not the time to check your iPhone. You want to be all attention and all smiles all the time.

## No "third-rail" topics

Watch your small talk. Politics, religion, and sex are always off limits. Stay in the positive — speaking about the town or city, building — absolutely anything involving the audience.

## Greet everyone with a SMILE

Don't interrupt your presentation, but do smile at late-comers and gesture for them to have a seat. If you're speaking to a large audience and chairs are scarce, you may want to stop to ask those sitting next to an empty seat to let you know by raising a hand. Locating spare seats will allow the maximum number of people to be seated.

## Be in control

As the presenter, you have the responsibility of keeping the audience quiet. I know, I know, you're also the guest; you don't want to offend anyone or make anybody mad. Unfortunately, if one or two or even a small group of people are talking, people around them won't be able to hear you, and that's what they came for. It's your job to make certain that everyone can hear you. And you have to do it in a friendly, almost invisible way. Putting your finger to your mouth and going, "Shhhh!" won't cut it.

Instead, you can use a more subtle and a way less humiliating but equally effective method. First, realize that the cross talkers may have no idea they're bothering those around them. In fact, they may not realize they're talking while someone else (you) is talking. Simply catch their eye and smile. That's all you have to do.

Nine times out of ten they'll smile back at you, possibly make a kind of "Oops" gesture, and you'll go on with your presentation. If they are repeat offenders, you may have to take a more aggressive approach.

If they seem to be intent on carrying on a conversation while you're talking and if you can move your body closer to them, do it. I'm not kidding. Move yourself closer to them without looking at them. Here's how it works. As you move closer, the audience follows you with their eyes. And as you move closer to the talkers, the audience's eyes look in their direction. The talkers feel you coming toward them and eyes on them, and, well, the jig is up. Works every time.

### Use your best manners

"Please" and "Thank you" and "May I?" go a long way. Look everyone you come in contact with in the eye. SMILE.

### Leave no trace

Always leave the stage, boardroom, or meeting room better than you found it. Straighten chairs, pick up garbage, replace markers for the white board. Be careful where you place your water bottle or coffee cup. You don't want to leave a water mark on a boardroom table as your calling card.

### Send a handwritten thank-you note

If you've been given the opportunity to present at a conference, a company meeting, or even at a sales presentation, sending a short handwritten note to whoever invited you to speak is a terrific goodwill gesture. Always a good thing.

## Take Aways

- Dress one level of formality above those to whom you'll be presenting.

- Turn off all electronic devices not being used in the presentation, and put them away.

- Remember that you are ON from the minute you enter the property. Act accordingly.

- Stay away from third-rail topics: politics, religion, sex.

- Greet everyone with a smile.

- Control your audience.

- Remember your manners.

- Clean up after yourself.

- Send a handwritten thank you.

Nail It.

---

# Presenting in Teams

The following are some good guidelines for presenting in teams. (With a shout-out to Lisa St. Germain and the good people at Open Solutions for many of these suggestions.)

### No time for fun and games

Politely introduce your fellow presenters. No inside jokes, no poking fun. Audiences don't like to feel as though they're on the outside looking in. Plus, what seems funny to your team may seem insulting to your audience. Worse, it may diminish one of the presenters in their eyes.

### Attention!

Pay attention to your fellow presenter while he or she is speaking. It looks painfully awkward, and impolite, to see one team member speaking while the others look straight ahead, down at their hands, at their iPhones . . . DO NOT be looking at, writing on, or playing with your laptop, phone, pager, or anything else while the presentation is in progress. Absolutely positively do not engage in conversation with others while a fellow presenter is speaking. All such behaviors show a disinterest in your fellow presenter. You want the audience to focus on your teammate. You need to set an example.

### Show respect

Do not interrupt your fellow presenter. Instead, ask for permission to speak. Something like, "Jim, may I interject something here?" works well. Along those lines, do not directly disagree with a fellow presenter. Offer an alternative view this way, "To tag on to what Jane was just saying, I think she'd agree that . . ." If you've arrived after the presentation has begun, beware of adding your own comments. You may be repeating something the presenter has said or stating something the presenter is about to say. Best to be quiet and observe. Don't catch a fellow presenter off guard. Let the presenter know ahead of time that you'll be asking him or her for input throughout your part of the presentation. Do NOT insult or criticize a fellow speaker EVER. You are a unified team. One big happy family. Keep your opinions to yourself.

## Don't create unnecessary distractions

DO NOT leave the room unless absolutely necessary. This means no going in and out of the room to answer calls, texts, emails. Also, apologies are BIG distractions for the audience. "I'm afraid I'm not as knowledgeable as my partner Tom" is nobody's business but yours. Likewise, "I'm not as charismatic a speaker" is for them to judge. (They'll probably find your calm manner a welcome change after Mr. Energy. )

## Practice beforehand

Each presenter should know exactly what he or she will be presenting, how one will "hand off" to the next, and how you'll handle Q & A. This means having a run-through in advance with slides, introductions, and other details.

## Be ready to help your fellow presenter

He or she may need you to elaborate on a point or help with a handout or change PowerPoint decks. These tasks should all be performed courteously and effortlessly. During Q & A, if you see a fellow presenter struggling with a question, offer to help answer it. (Again, this means paying attention the whole time.)

Nail It.

### Be aware of your audience

If you see they're tiring, make your segment shorter, hit the high points, and move toward the conclusion. If you see confused looks, stop your fellow presenter and ask him or her to explain. If you hear murmuring that audience members can't see a chart or can't hear a presenter, let him or her know. Having more eyes and ears should make your team that much more able to discern your audience's engagement, understanding, and saturation level.

---

## Take Aways

- No inside jokes.

- Pay attention to your fellow presenters — no cross talk or iPhone surfing.

- Give your fellow presenters the respect you want them to give you.

- Don't create distractions for the audience.

- Practice as a group beforehand.

- Be there for your fellow presenters.

- Be aware of the audience. Be ready to jump in to clarify or to signal a speaker to cut the presentation short if need be.

# Questions and Answers (Q and A)

As I mentioned earlier, unless your audience is relatively small (under twenty-five people), you'll want to hold questions until the end of your presentation. Why? Larger audiences can mean more questions, and the more questions, the less likely you are to get through your prepared content. Presenters I work with often tell me they would like to be "interactive." I'm a big fan of audience participation, but that's not the same thing as turning control of your presentation over to your audience. It may feel better to toss the focus to them (and take it away from you), but remember, your audience members came to hear you speak about a certain topic. They'll not be pleased if things go off the rails and you end up never really getting to your prepared remarks.

## No hi-jacking

Let your audience know at the outset that you'll be taking questions at the end of the presentation. I always include the caveat that if I say something they don't understand, I'd like them to stop me so that I can explain. This works well. I don't run the risk of losing anyone who may be confused, and I also don't run the risk of having my presentation hi-jacked by a well-meaning questioner.

When you get to the end of your presentation, let them know how much time you have for questions. This helps people self-moderate. If you've allotted substantial time for questions, you'll want to have a "plant" in the room prepared to ask a question or two if your audience is shy. If that's not possible, you can always say something like, "Often I'm asked . . ." and then ask yourself a question. If you've planned a lot of time for Q and A, you might even break the audience into small groups and have them come up with questions. No matter what, always give a little space for that first question. I know it may feel awkward to stand there in silence, but someone always raises his or her hand. And once that first hand is raised, others typically follow.

Be sure to reward that first brave soul who raises his or her hand. There are plenty of sincere ways to do this. A simple, "Thanks so much for asking that" works well. I often find that audience members will ask a question about something I had meant to address but had forgotten. I always enthusiastically thank them for prompting me to share something I'd missed.

## Not knowing is okay

If you don't know the answer to a particular question, don't worry about it. Simply admit that you don't know the answer, but if they'll give you their contact information, you'll be happy to get back to them with the answer. Audiences don't expect you to know or even remember everything. They just want to get the information they seek. Don't forget to follow up with them. That seemingly small act will go a long, long way.

## Ruh roh: The inevitable blank-out

Likewise with an answer you should know, you know you know, but darned if you aren't drawing a complete and total blank. Who cares? In fact, confessing that you're having a "senior moment" makes you more human and thus more approachable. (And chances are the answer will come to you before the Q and A segment is over.)

## Involve everyone

Address the entire audience when you're answering a question — not just the person who asked it. This will help everyone stay connected to you during the Q and A. You've probably had the experience of being in an audience that devolved into chaos once the speaker began answering questions. This is usually because the speaker makes the mistake of engaging in intense one-on-one conversations with each questioner, and the rest of the audience feels left out. They then tune out and engage in one-on-one conversations with one another. Voila! Chaos. Instead, make eye contact with various people around the room, and then conclude your answer looking at your questioner.

## Repeat after me

With groups larger than twenty-five people, always repeat a question before you answer it. Audiences will become frustrated quickly if they don't know what your answer is in response to. (This is unnecessary if audience members are provided with a microphone and you're sure they can be heard.)

## Long, involved answers

If a particular question requires a lengthy response, find a way to answer it briefly and suggest the questioner see you afterward for a more in-depth answer. This will keep the Q and A lively and give others a chance to ask their questions. If, however, the question is regarding an important topic that you feel everyone would benefit from hearing about in detail, go for it.

## Overeager questioners

Don't let a particularly enthusiastic audience member monopolize the Q and A period. My rule is two questions max per questioner. If you can see that the person is itching to ask yet another question, acknowledge his or her interest in the subject and suggest you continue the conversation after the presentation ends. Then look to an opposite part of the room and ask, "Who else has a question?"

## Audience eruptions

If an answer to a question seems to ignite audience cross talk, wait for the noise to die down before either commenting or asking another question. Don't shout over your audience! Don't panic. Smile and wait. Cross talk is a good thing. It means you hit a nerve, struck a collective interest, or caused conflict. Ultimately it means your audience is engaged. That's never a bad thing.

### Tough questions

If someone asks a question that requires a carefully considered response, buy time by repeating the question. You can even preface this with some kind of pre-answer: "That's not a question I'm asked often" or "I want to be sure I answer this carefully so there's no confusion." This will create the space for your brain to construct a well-thought-out answer.

### Hostile and emotional questions and questioners

Every once in a while someone will ask a question that feels confrontational or even downright hostile. First, smile. Take a deep breath and begin by acknowledging the confronter's point of view. Remember, all of us want to be heard. If at all possible, respond without using the word *but.* You can leave *but* out and still get your point across. (That you politely disagree.) DO NOT fold your arms over your chest, get in the confronter's space, frown, or raise your voice.

This goes for emotional questioners as well. Smile, speak in a low tone, evenly measured, but not condescending. (That will only send them into orbit.) Acknowledge politely their point of view, validating it if you can. "I can see how you would feel that way" or "Yes, I hear that objection quite a bit." These statements, coupled with your supercalm demeanor, should defuse their emotion. They may even look embarrassed, apologize, or step all over themselves agreeing with you. Your goal is to agree to disagree and allow them to maintain their dignity while you maintain yours.

### Give 'em the five-minute warning

As the ending time for your presentation approaches, let the audience know you have time for just a few more questions. Again they will self-select. Those who feel they have a pressing question will continue to raise their hands. Others will put their hands down, deciding to ask their question afterward or possibly write you about it. End by thanking them and whoever invited you. Remind them you'll stick around to chat with whoever still has a question or comment. They should have easy access to your contact information, either on a PowerPoint slide, a handout, or your business card. Always be sure they have avenues to keep the conversation going.

## Take Aways

- For audiences of more than twenty-five people, take questions at the conclusion of your presentation.

- Don't be worried if you don't know the answer to a question. Let the audience know you'll get back to them with the answer.

- Likewise, don't worry about drawing a blank. Let it go — it'll come back to you.

- Speak to everyone when answering the question.

- Always repeat the question unless the questioner is speaking into the microphone and can be heard by the entire group.

- Don't get into "deep dives" during Q and A. Answer briefly and encourage the questioner to seek you out afterward.

- If the audience erupts in cross talk, SMILE, and wait for it to die down.

- Repeat the question if it's a tough one and you need a minute to come up with the answer.

- Remember, "low and slow" for emotional questioners. Listen and acknowledge their point of view.

Nail It.


- Let the audience know when you hit the five-minute mark; they'll decide whether their question is important enough to be answered before time's up.

- Always be sure to provide the audience easy access to you, both in the immediate and distant future.

# Practice

You've got your presentation together, you've created your visual aids, you're good to go, right? Not so fast there, Flash. You're missing a critical component to successful public speaking: practice. Mark Twain said the best extemporaneous speeches require hours of practice. Boy, was he right. There is absolutely, positively, no substitute for practice, and no way to be a truly good, effective speaker without it.

And by "practice" I do NOT mean sitting at your desk or at home in your pj's clicking through your PowerPoint slides. You must practice OUT LOUD. In your head doesn't count. How many times have you practiced something in your head and thought, "Wow! That sounds pretty great!" only to say it to a room full of real, live people and think, "IDIOT! What were you thinking?!? That sounds moronic!" Yeah, exactly. Trust me, there is nothing scarier than standing up in front of a group of people hearing words come out of your mouth for the very first time.

## Perfect Places To Practice

Think you don't have time to practice? I have two words for you: shower and car. We all take a shower at least every other day, and we are all alone in our cars for at least fifteen minutes a day. Both are excellent places to practice.

The shower is perfect; the acoustics are great! While you're washing your hair, run through your introduction and the transition to your first point. And again, this practice must be done OUT LOUD. In your head absolutely does not count. Period.

The car is an excellent place to practice as well, and with the advent of all kinds of fabulous new technology that allows you to talk hands free in your car, no one needs to know you are talking only to yourself. Turn off the radio and run through your last point and conclusion. I recommend putting a digital recorder in your car (you can also use your cell phone) to record whatever you're saying. That way you can play it back to hear how it sounds. Often something we thought would be great sounds pretty dull when we hear it played back, and something we toss out without really thinking about it ends up being a home run. We have no way of really knowing which is which unless we hear it ourselves.

### It's about what you say, not how you sound

By the way, audio is a lot like video. We inevitably "hate" the way our voices sound. You must listen to yourself on tape enough to get over the sound of your voice and get to what's more important, namely, what it is you're saying. If you do find yourself excessively monotone or nasal or quiet, try modulating your voice accordingly.

The first time you practice your presentation OUT LOUD, you probably will get through only the first few minutes before you find yourself stuck. You'll realize you don't have a transition between the introduction and your first main point, or you'll find that the first main point should probably be the third point. Often we discover we're missing something altogether or we've put something in that doesn't belong. Don't panic. This is exactly what's supposed to happen the first time through. That's why you practice OUT LOUD. Going through your presentation from beginning to end OUT LOUD is the only way to learn what works and what doesn't, what's missing, and what doesn't fit. And this is exactly the time and place to find out, before you're actually giving your presentation to a room full of real, live people.

### Practice, practice, practice

Once you've made it through the entire presentation and everything works, go through it at least twice more to really get it down. I recommend practicing the introduction until you know it cold.

Why? First, because it is the most critical part of the presentation. The audience is sizing you up, you're laying out the framework of what you'll be talking about, setting the stage. Second, this is when you'll be most nervous. We've all experienced this (even big ol' hams like me). The first few minutes of your presentation are almost an out-of-body experience. If you know what you're saying inside out and backward, you can allow your mouth to go on autopilot and give yourself a chance to climb back into your own body. With a successful introduction under your belt, you feel confident and in control. Now you can really take off, possibly even ad-lib a little bit, and thoroughly enjoy your presentation.

## Take Aways

- Videotaping, recording, or just plain talking to yourself, you MUST practice, and you must practice OUT LOUD. In your head doesn't count.

- Run through your presentation at least two times once you've got it all nailed down.

- Give your speech to a room full of furniture or file cabinets or in the shower or car. The reward is well worth it.

If you take nothing else away from this book except the importance of practice, you'll be an exponentially better speaker. Guaranteed. You'll find yourself in front of a group of people speaking in a much more confident, compelling way, fully in control and in the moment because you've practiced. You'll nail it every time.

# 5
# Logistics

Now that you've built and rehearsed you audience-focused presentation, you're ready to get out there and deliver it. Before you get to the site on the big day you'll want to be certain you've got all the particulars squared away. Here's what to get figured out way before you show up to give your presentation.

## Let them know what you need ahead of time

In a perfect world, your host will contact you well in advance to ask what your audiovisual requirements will be. If not, make sure you let him or her know at least a few weeks before. Do NOT assume they'll have a projector, an extension cord, a table for your handouts, or a glass of water for you. You know what you're planning to bring. Make sure they're prepared to supply the rest.

## And vice versa

If they've asked you to submit your PowerPoint deck or your handouts or your bio, do so promptly. Don't make them ask you more than once. You want to make a great impression from start to finish. A good way to guarantee you won't be invited back to speak is to (a) be demanding at the last minute, (b) be unresponsive to their requests for information, or (c) be high maintenance.

# The Bespeak LOGISTICS ASSESSMENT TOOL

Here are some good questions to ask of whoever has asked you to speak. You can certainly add some of your own to this short list. The idea is to be as well prepared as possible for what you will encounter on the day of the presentation.

## IS THIS A FORMAL PRESENTATION SETTING OR A CASUAL ONE?

Are you going to be addressing a group of "suits" or men and women ready to go play eighteen holes of golf? Your style and demeanor should match theirs but be more deferential. In other words, if they'll be in khakis and polo shirts, you should be in a sport coat and a button-down shirt. If they wear sport coats, you should wear a suit.

## TIME OF DAY?
### (EARLY MORNING, AFTER LUNCH, LATE AFTERNOON)

This is SO important, yet many presenters don't give it any consideration. If you are the only speaker, or you're coming in to pitch your idea or product, you can have some influence on the day and time. Use it! Monday mornings aren't ideal; people usually have a ton of work they want to get done that they've been thinking about all weekend. Thursday would be my pick. The weekend's in sight, and people tend to be more relaxed and amenable to new ideas. Fridays they may be itching to get out the door or preoccupied with what they'll do once they get there, or worse, preoccupied thinking about all they need to get done before they can get out the door. (You may be thinking this is a lot to consider. You're right, but I'm trying to load you for success here. The more thoughtful beforehand, the better your odds of success.)

## WHERE ARE YOU IN THE LINE-UP?

If you're speaking at a conference, you'll want to know ahead of time where you are in the lineup. If you are the first speaker of the day you will be responsible for setting the tone. Make it lively, but not jarring. In fact, if you are given the option of choosing a time to speak, being first is my recommendation. (Unless the conference day starts really, really early and you know people will have been up late socializing the night before. In that case, you want to be the second speaker of the morning.) Being the first or

### Don't Let Respectful Get in the Way of Connecting

Be careful, however, not to be too far above them apparel-wise. One of my favorite clients, Ed Laflamme, an author and landscape business consultant, was accustomed to wearing his best, most expensive (and I mean expensive) suits and ties when presenting to landscapers. Always gracious, Ed's objective was to show the audience his highest level of respect. In past presentations he'd even gone so far as to tell his audience how pricey his tie was (with a nod to his wife, whom he credited with buying it for him) as a way of showing his audience how important they were to him.

Best intentions aside, this was not a great way to connect with his audience. For the most part, landscape business owners are down-to-earth, hard-working folks. They don't relate to $500 ties. We agreed that he would begin his presentation wearing nice slacks and a sport coat, but that as soon as his introduction was over, he'd say, "Okay, let's get down to work." And he'd take the coat off and roll up his sleeves. This would let the audience know he respected them (higher level of dress) but that he understood them and was, in fact, one of them (taking off the sport coat and adopting a more worklike attire).

second speaker of the day is great for a couple of reasons. First, everyone is awake. Second, their "listeners" aren't worn out. Listening is hard, hard work. Being one of the first speakers gives you much better odds of being heard and remembered. Plus, if you're one of the first speakers on the first day, there's virtually no chance you'll be saying something they've already heard. YOU get to set the tone, give the first ideas. You are the presenter the other presenters will be measured against.

## If their stomachs are rumbling . . .

If you are speaking just before lunch, do NOT go long (people are hungry!). And if the speakers before you went long, you will have to truncate your own material. I know, I know, it's not fair. You researched your audience, practiced and practiced, and now you have to leave a big portion of your beloved presentation on the cutting-room floor at the last minute — and all because of those windbags who came before you! (Another reason, ahem, you want to be the first or second speaker of the day.) Sorry, my friend. That's show biz. You cannot punish an audience (or their stomachs), because previous presenters don't know how to plan or tell time. The audience has been polite and attentive all morning, and now they want (and need and deserve) a break and the opportunity to stretch their legs, chat, and call home or the office. Their needs have to come before your own. Go short. Be careful, however. Never to go too, too short. You don't want to put the food and beverage people into a tailspin because you were supposed to speak until twelve thirty and you ended at eleven thirty. A good rule of thumb is to get them out for lunch no more than fifteen minutes early.

### It's nap time!

If you're speaking just after lunch you'll have to be VERY energetic. This is the sleepiest time of day for conference attendees. All their energy is in their stomachs digesting their food. You may even want to incorporate more than your usual audience interaction to keep them on their toes — truly. And by all means, if you have the misfortune to be the last speaker of the day, "Run for the barn," as they say in show biz (make it short and sweet). Let the audience know at the outset that although you'd been scheduled to speak for an hour and fifteen minutes, you were pretty sure everyone would prefer to get to cocktails, so you've decided to shorten your comments to forty-five minutes. Let them know you LOVE to talk about this subject and that they should grab you during cocktail hour or dinner and you'll be happy to answer questions. You'll be an instant hero! Get the cape!

## ARE YOU THE ONLY SPEAKER?

If you are the only speaker, your life is easier and your responsibility is greater. You do not have the worries of another speaker stealing your thunder. You do, however, need to have a cogent, complete, compelling presentation. You also need to get there early and stay late. I don't mean late-like-the-custodian late, but you need to stay long enough to answer questions, chat with people. Why? First, there may be people who want to ask you a question one on one, or comment on an aspect of what you said or even thank you in person. Sticking around shows the audience you're open to this kind of interaction and, more important, that you're eager and interested to hear what they have to say.

### Learn about the other speakers

You should design your presentation with an idea of how you fit into the "big picture." If you are one of a few or one of many, find out what topics the other speakers are presenting. You may even want to go to each of their websites to get an idea of what their style is like. DO NOT try to imitate their style or panic that you're not like them. Diversity is a good thing. If the speaker before you is supermanic and your style is more reserved, not to worry. The audience will welcome someone moving at a more relaxed speed after Mr. Frenetic.

The day of the presentation you must get to the site of your presentation early, ready to present if those before you go short, or worse, a presenter doesn't show. You'll want to pay close attention to how those before you deliver and how they're received. If they've been lackluster, turn it up a notch or two, get the audience's attention, and keep it. You also need to be there to see the other presenters to avoid repeating something they've said. Better yet, having heard what the audience has heard, you can use this material and tie it to your presentation. This cohesiveness will help your audience not only tie important concepts together, it will make you a better, more relevant speaker in their eyes. Equally important, it shows interest in them, something they'll truly appreciate.

### Be attentive and flexible

If you are first, you set the tone. Make your presentation energized, enthusiastic, and memorable. (You should do this no matter where you are in the lineup.) If, however, you are fourth or fifth in line, you may have to shorten your remarks if audience energy is low or attention is fading. If it's clear they've had all the talk they can handle, you'll serve them better by letting them go than by trying to stuff their poor brains with more information.

Remember, timewise, if the speakers before you have all run late, try to make up the time difference — the audience will thank you for it. DO NOT try to "get your time in." This will only aggravate or even anger them and bring more stress to the conference organizers, who are desperate to make the trains run on time. Suck it up, and shorten your presentation. Everyone will be grateful to you for it.

How to do this? It's a good idea to think of a "skinny" version of your presentation. What would a slimmed-down version look like? What are the real key points you want to get across? How can you do that in two-thirds of the time allotted? Half the time? Prepare your presentation for this eventuality just in case. It's a good practice to have an hour version, a forty-five-minute version, a thirty-minute version, and a twenty-minute version of your presentation. Figure out how each of those would work. You'll always be glad you did.

## Scope out the room

Another reason to get to the site of your presentation well in advance is so that you can get comfortable with the size and shape of the space in which you'll be speaking. More than once I've been surprised by the dimensions, layout, lighting, resources, and acoustics in a room.

Nail It.

### A Circus Tent in a Prison

Well, actually, it was a "room" in a convention center at a business expo, my first-ever experience presenting at a BIG business expo. I was over the moon about the opportunity (think the biggest city in the country) but more than a little intimidated by the layout. The conference center was the size of multiple football fields, built of concrete. My "presentation room" was two hundred folding chairs surrounded by a heavy curtain. On either side of me were other "presentation rooms." I had a hand-held microphone in which to shout (so as not to be drowned out by my fellow presenters on either side). For visibility for those way in the back? My tiptoes. Luckily, I'd arrived at the venue two hours ahead of time so that I could see the presenter before me. I made note of where he stood, how closely he held the microphone to his mouth, and how easily I could see and hear him. Although the logistics were less than optimal, I was as prepared as I could be when I took the "stage."

Things like visibility (can they see you?) and acoustics (can they hear you?) are critical. You MUST be able to be seen and heard by everyone. Once people can't see or hear you, they'll start talking among themselves, and then all is lost. A clue: if you begin speaking and you hear lots of rumbling, chances are they're saying to one another, "Can you hear him? I can't hear him." STOP, and make sure everyone in the room can hear you before moving on. If you're not sure you can be heard or seen, ASK. Then correct the problem before moving on. This is a non-negotiable deal-breaker. An audience that can't hear you will devolve into chaos in a matter of minutes.

If they provide a microphone, use it unless you have a big booming voice. I am a small person with a BIG sound. I often opt not to use a mic, but I always always ask whether everyone can hear me before I begin my presentation. If you are presenting with someone else and he or she doesn't need a microphone, you must still use one if you are not loud enough on your own.

If they have more than one type of microphone, opt for the one that gives you the most visibility and freedom of movement, typically a lavalier (clip-on) mic. You do not want to use a podium mic unless there is no other alternative; podiums create a barrier between you and your audience. (Yes, I know, Mr. Nervous Speaker, you love the podium because it gives you something to grip, a feeling of security. I can hear you now, "What's so bad about a barrier, anyway?" There's nothing wrong with standing behind a podium if you're not interested in connecting with your audience.) Having said all this, nothing trumps hearability. That is your number one concern.

## Rearranging furniture

If there's a podium at the center of the stage and you'll not be using one, ask whether it can be moved offstage or out of the way. If there's a table for a panel that has presented before you or will speak after you, ask whether it's possible to move it back. I've often rearranged the chairs at round tables so that people won't have to be sitting with their backs to me. Call me a control freak, but I am always working for optimum audience receptivity. No one can get really bent out of shape about that. That said, you want to be unceasingly polite. If you ask for something to be moved and the answer is no, smile and assure your host it's not a problem.

Nail It.

> ### Don't Be a Nightmare "Guest"
>
> While I'm a big fan of having the site of my presentation the way I want it, I am very, very careful not to step on any toes. You want to be on your best "presenter manners." This means asking politely for any changes you'd like to see and even helping to move things around. It also means smiling broadly if things can't be set up to your liking. (Remember, you are the guest, and you want to be invited back.) Be sure you comply with all requests for materials: your bio and your PowerPoint deck, for example. You do NOT want to cause problems, especially on the day of the presentation. Just the opposite, you want to be the easiest, friendliest, most self-sufficient presenter your hosts have ever encountered.

## Logistics: Small Venues and Small Audiences

Many of the same elements apply when preparing to speak to a smaller group. Typically the venue will be some type of conference room or meeting room. Don't assume anything. Contact those in charge of your presentation well ahead of time to eliminate any unwelcome surprises. For example, in addition to the audience assessment, you'll want to ask about the shape and set-up of the room, what AV equipment it has, connection to the Internet if you need it, and details like that.

### Get there early

Ask whether you can get there thirty minutes early. When you arrive, be sure to test your visuals (PowerPoint, Internet connection). If the room set-up is not to your liking, ask politely whether it would be all right to move a few things. Explain your reasoning. If it's your first or second visit, be very judicious about these requests. They should be made only insofar as they will enhance the audience's experience.

### Send what they ask for, but with caveats

Be sure that you've sent anything your hosts have requested promptly. I recommend, however, that you ask them not to share any of your visual aids or handouts with audience members ahead of time. The exception to this is presentations to board members, who typically insist on reading materials in advance of presentations. In this case, you'll have two PowerPoint decks, one that is rich in information and sent ahead of time, and another that you'll use to present, which will act as a visual aid (more on that in the chapter on visual aids) and NOT as reading material.

### Keep the space tidy

Be sure to keep your presentation area tidy—no piles of files, purses, cell phones. Your laptop or tablet should be visible only when it's used in the presentation. There's usually a place either under the table or at the back of the room to hide your other things.

### Be mindful of time of day

You'll want to be cognizant of the time of day as well. Before lunch or before the end of the business day, you'll want to go a little short (speak for a shorter amount of time) of your allotted time. If there is great interest in your presentation, your hosts may choose to extend your session. This is obviously a good thing, but always up to your hosts.

## Take Aways

- Know as much as you possibly can about the logistics of your presentation venue before you get there.

- Be prepared to "go short" if the speakers before you have exceeded their time slots.

- What will the room look like?

- Will there be equipment you need?

- What's the best way to get your visual aids and collateral materials there?

- If you'll be speaking at a conference, what time of day will you be speaking?

- Are you the sole presenter or one of many?

- If you're one of a group, who is speaking before you?

- What are their topics?

- What is their speaking style?

Knowing the answers to these questions will enable you to be prepared and flexible when the big day arrives and you're giving the presentation. You'll be able to adjust your tempo, timing, and energy level to suit the circumstances.

# 6
# Nerves

## Let's Talk about Fear

For many of you reading this book, the only thing you can really focus on is your pounding heart, sweaty palms, and shaking hands. Being a better presenter? You'd settle for being a happier, calmer presenter. You'd love to be able to sleep the night before a presentation, to be in control of yourself while you're presenting, to actually remember what you said in the presentation. Am I right?

This section of the book is for you. We'll address a lot of the same things — being yourself, audience assessment, preparation, practice — but all with an eye toward helping you become a confident, calm, composed speaker. It absolutely can be done. I know it can because I've helped hundreds of fearful people get in front of audiences and LOVE the experience (and want to do it again).

As you read through these tips, think positively about how they can help you. Lots of studying has been done about the brain and its inability to differentiate between what actually happens in our lives and our perceptions or predictions of what happened or will happen. Start telling yourself NOW, right this minute, that you're a confident, compelling speaker. Let it bring up a good, positive feeling. Hang on to it, refer to it, carry it with you, and you will make it a reality.

## Fear and Focus

As I stated earlier, even the most confident speakers feel nervous when they first stand up to speak. This is a normal, typical physical reaction to standing or even sitting and speaking to a group. The difference for fearful speakers is that they focus on this initial physical reaction.

It goes something like this. You stand up to speak and your heart pounds. As you begin speaking, you focus on your pounding heart. Now you start to sweat. "Oh my God," you're thinking, "I'm sweating. Everyone can see me sweating. My heart is pounding so hard I swear everyone in the room can hear it. Now I'm sweating more. This is so humiliating . . ." Your eyes dart around the room. You feel as though you're under siege. What are you even talking about anyway? You have no idea, you're too busy focusing on yourself and your fear. Sound familiar?

If this is you, believe it or not, you are actually contributing to your own horrible speaking experience. The more you focus on your fear, the more you feed it, encourage it, accelerate it, and aggravate it. You perpetuate a vicious cycle: the more you think about your fear, the worse it gets.

Michael Motley, a professor at UC Davis, is an expert on this subject. He has done extensive research about fear and public speaking. His book *Overcoming Your Fear of Public Speaking* is a no-nonsense explanation of the "why'" of this fear and the "how-to's" of conquering it.

## Motley's Three Reactions

According to Dr. Motley, there are three reactions we all experience in the presentation process. He outlines these reactions in more detail in his book; I've summarized them here. The first he calls the Anticipation Reaction, which occurs a few minutes before we are about to speak. Here, heart rates elevate to what can be, for a moderately anxious or very anxious speaker, an uncomfortable feeling: from around 95 beats per minute (bpm) to 140. (A resting bpm is somewhere in the 70s.)

Next comes the "Confrontation Reaction," when the speaker stands to speak and faces the audience. Motley says that we experience a rush of adrenaline, and heart rates can surge to more than 180 beats per minute. Fortunately, better news comes with the third of Motley's phases. The "Adaptation Reaction" is when our bodies get used to the idea of standing in front of a group of people and speaking, and our heart rate slows down, typically within the first sixty seconds of speaking.

For anxious speakers, the Confrontation Reaction is so memorable (and not in a good way) that, Motley says, they are convinced it's lasted through the entire presentation. Here's where he says they can help themselves: begin noticing that your body does, in fact, become accustomed to standing before a group and speaking. Notice that your heart rate does, in fact, slow down. Motley also asks us to remember that presentations are acts of communication, NOT performance. Orienting your thoughts around this concept is critical, he says. Public speaking is about getting your point across, not about being a comedian or magician or entertainer. I could not agree more.

Especially in a business setting, your goal is to communicate your message in the clearest, most compelling way possible. In fact, often the success of your company or your career will rest on your ability to communicate, NOT your ability to entertain or amuse. Communication is all about getting your message across to others.

It's way more about them than about you. Which brings us back to one of my favorite Bespeakisms:

## Turn Your Focus 180°

Turning your focus 180° is a WINNING strategy for the nervous speaker. You know by now my commitment to the audience. Turning your focus 180° is key for them, and for YOU. The whole purpose of the presentation, any presentation, is to get a message to an audience. When the nervous speaker makes the 180° turn and focuses on the audience and getting his message across to them, he stops focusing on himself and his nerves. That is a win-win.

As I said at the beginning of this chapter, focusing on your nerves only makes them more pronounced. What do you think would happen if you learned to ignore them? Exactly, your body would do what Motley's studies have proved: your heart rate would return to a comfortable level and your body along with it. The next time you find yourself in front of an audience and you hear yourself saying to yourself, "Here I go. My hands are shaking, I'm sweating. I hate this," STOP. Tell yourself, "Wrong focus!" Shake your head clear, and concentrate on the audience and on getting your message across to them. Focus all your attention on connecting with them. After all, that's why you're there. More important, that's why the audience is there.

### Nervous? Nobody cares.

Public speaking is a dynamic, real-time thing. The more you can connect with your audience, the more thrilling it will be for them and the more memorable. They should have your absolute 100% undivided attention. Remember, they are your guests. They are your number-one priority. They are what matter. You? You're merely the vehicle through which the message is transmitted. Pretty inconsequential to them. (No offense.)

In fact, studies have been done to determine how much of a presenter's nervous behavior an audience really sees. Wanna take a guess? Only 2% to 3 % of what the speaker is absolutely convinced she's exhibiting. You know why they don't see it? Because they don't care. They're not there to evaluate your speaking skills or level of nerves. They're there to learn something, be convinced of something, do something. So quit thinking about yourself. Stop worrying that the audience can see you sweating (they can't). Focus on what's really important: getting your message across to them.

### Set yourself up for success: Start EARLY

It's pretty much human nature to avoid things we don't like. "If only," we think, "I can ignore it, put it off, pretend it doesn't exist, surely it will go away." I am always reminded of a story about my brother-in-law, who, at age three, put his hands over his eyes and proclaimed, "God can't see me!" Uh, not exactly. Chances are the presentation will still have to be given (and given by you) on the scheduled date whether you choose to ignore it or not. The best thing you can do for yourself and your comfort level is to get started as early as possible to give yourself plenty of time to assess your audience, develop your presentation, and to PRACTICE IT OUT LOUD.

## Organizing Your Material: A Few Key DON'T's

The way you organize your material is also a critical factor in abating nerves. Here are a few methods that DO NOT help you diminish nerves or get your message across. If you are using one of these, I beg you to take a deep breath and cease and desist. There's a better way!

Nail It.

### Don't memorize

Memorizing is a bad idea, and Michael Motley backs me up. First, because if you forget a "line" mid-speech, it will absolutely send you into a tailspin (and searching for the nearest exit). Second, it comes out sounding wooden and *memorized*. I want you to practice and be intimately familiar with your material, but memorize? No way.

### Don't create (and read from or refer to) a script

Using a script. Another suicidal method. How are you going to keep your place? (Can you imagine how nervous you'd be if you lost your place in front of a real live audience?) Are you just going to read the whole thing? Bad idea. It's virtually impossible to come across as sincere while you're reading. Are you a famous script writer? If not, it's going to sound like you're reciting, not like you're talking, even if you do only glance at it once in a while.

### Don't create any kind of notes for yourself that require reading

Again, you don't want to run the risk of losing your place, sounding inauthentic or insincere. Instead, make a list of trigger thoughts, billboards, bullets. These should be short phrases you can look at and immediately know where you're going next. Don't worry if it doesn't come out the same way every time. It shouldn't. It's not a performance; it's a communication. A structured idea you're presenting to an audience. As long as you hit the important stuff, you're batting a thousand.

### Don't create text-intensive slides

Here's why text-intensive slides are bad for you. If it's up on the screen, you'll be forced to address it (assuming you're not going to commit the absolutely unforgivable sin of reading the darn thing). You have now locked yourself into talking about every bullet and piece of information on the slides. Plus, you have to keep looking at the slides to remind yourself where you are and where you're going. Better have a hearty constitution. That kind of head swinging can make a person seasick.

It's bad for the audience because if everything you're going to say is up on the screen, they're going to read the screen and then get real fidgety real fast. (Remember, they can read somewhere between three to ten times faster than you can speak.) Seeing them squirm, fiddle with stuff, and whisper to one another is not going to help your nerves one bit.

Here's the good news about PowerPoint. It is a visual, and visual aids help us remember things. If you've practiced your presentation with your PowerPoint deck, the visuals will jog your memory and keep you on track. You don't need tons of bullets with every minute detail displayed.

You may, however, need little reminders. Again, think billboards. Just a word or phrase will work. You can put these on index cards, on a sheet of paper, whatever works. Please make sure they are easy to read. Cursive is usually not a good idea. Fourteen-point type, double spaced, in a plain font like Arial works best. Keep it simple. And BIG.

## The Biggest, Biggest Help to Nervous Speakers

You should PRACTICE OUT LOUD a lot. (Okay, you're rolling your eyes right now because you've read this already in a previous chapter. I don't care. PRACTICING OUT LOUD is the single most important thing a nervous speaker can do. The more nervous you are, the more practice you need.)

Which means you must begin building your presentation allowing plenty of time for practice. DO NOT panic if the first time through feels like Mr. Toad's Wild Ride. Fix what needs to be fixed and try it again. And again. I want you to practice the complete presentation at least three times, and OUT LOUD, STANDING UP.

There are simply no number of times too many to practice your introduction and conclusion. Play with both of them, try different things. I'd like them both locked down with enough time to practice them over and over and over. Remember, during the introduction is when you'll be experiencing Motley's Confrontation Reaction. Having your introduction nailed down will allow your heart rate to slow that much faster. What's more, the better start you get off to, the more confident you'll feel as you get into the meat of the presentation. How great will that be?

## Setting Yourself up for Success

Now, let's take you to just before the presentation begins. You get there early. (And the more anxious a speaker you are, the more you must ENSURE you get there early. No less than thirty minutes before.) You will set up whatever you need to (projector, laptop, slide show, handouts) and then walk the room. Stand where you'll be standing when you present. BREATHE. Sit in a few of the seats provided for the audience. See what it will feel like for them, what it will look like from different places in the room. BREATHE. If a host or facilitator is there, thank him or her again for having you, engage them in conversation. DO NOT tell them how nervous you are or that you thought you had the date wrong or that you had a terrible time getting there. (All information he or she does not need to know.) Ask about the person, about the business or organization, about the audience. Remember, this is where your focus is supposed to be. Making sure it's there will give you less mental and emotional energy to worry about yourself and your nerves.

### Chat them up

As the audience enters, introduce yourself to a few of them. Smile. Make small talk. You are deputizing these people, signing them up for your fan club. They may not know it while you're chatting, but they'll feel it in their guts when you begin to speak. They'll be smiling at you and internally cheering you on.

## Smile!

As you stand up to speak, SMILE. Studies show that smiling has two great benefits. First, it makes us feel good physically. Second, when we smile at someone, they smile back. Now we're feeling good, and our audience is feeling good because they're now smiling and we're feeling even better because we're looking at faces smiling at us. (I know, this may sound like unicorns and rainbows, but do yourself a favor and try it. It works.) Thank whoever introduced you, whoever invited you. Let the audience know how grateful and glad you are to be speaking to them. Then begin.

## Don't apologize

Remember, if your slides are out of order or you forget to say something, DON'T APOLOGIZE. It doesn't matter. They'll never know, nor will they care. If you forgot to say something important, just say, "OH! I forgot to tell you this really important thing . . ." No harm done. No biggie. In fact, your ability to acknowledge casually that you left something out and you're now tagging back to it shows a confidence in yourself and a focus on giving them the information they came for.

## If you don't tell them, they won't know

Whatever you do, do NOT tell the audience you are nervous, or (at the conclusion) that you're so glad to be done with this presentation or that you're amazed you made it through without hyperventilating. NONE of this is their business. Remember, they are there to hear your message. They are not, nor should they be, concerned with your nerves. And if you don't tell them, they won't know!

Nail It.

## Take Aways

- Give yourself plenty of time to prepare and practice your presentation.

- Organize your material.

- DO NOT write a script.

- DO NOT READ slides, notes, scripts.

- DO NOT memorize. This will only make you sound wooden and put you in panic mode if you blank out.

- Get to the site of your presentation early.

- Meet and greet your audience. Make small talk.

- SMILE.

- Keep negative thoughts to yourself.

- PRACTICE OUT LOUD.

Follow these guidelines and you will be an exponentially less nervous speaker. I guarantee it. Over the years I have worked with hundreds of presenters, a large percentage of whom experienced serious presentation anxiety. Every one of them who followed these simple rules not only became way less nervous, they looked for and forward to opportunities to speak. These methods work.

# 7
# Step by Step

W e've gone through lots of tools, tips, guidelines, formats, and do's and don't's, from assessing the audience to building the presentation to assessing you as the presenter, checking out the location, meeting the audience, speaking, answering questions. At this point, your head may be swimming a little bit. I know mine does when I read too many "helpful how-to's."

So let's take this whole thing step by step. For the sake of the time line, we're going to assume that you've addressed any audience distracters and have got them under control. For those of you reading this who are nervous speakers, I'll point out steps in the time line to help combat nerves.

We'll begin at the point where you know you have an upcoming speaking engagement. I'd love to give you a real time frame to this time line. Unfortunately that wouldn't be realistic. Best-case scenario, you've got ninety days to prepare. More often it's more like thirty days, and sometimes it's as little as a week.

Nail It.

## Step 1: Assess Your Audience

Use the Audience Assessment tool to ask yourself — or whoever asked you to speak or knows the audience best — important questions about your audience. Keep this information in mind as you build your presentation. Remember, it can be the most well crafted thing ever created, but if it's not written with the audience in mind, in a language they can understand, addressing their needs and concerns, you may as well just give it to your dog and be done with it.

## Step 2: Brainstorm All Relevant Ideas

Write them down. Use whatever method works best for you. For some, a blank piece of construction paper (bigger than standard or even legal) helps. Others love the "mind map," with the main point in a circle in the center of the paper and connections to it with sub-ideas. Others will want to create lists. Whatever works best for you.

By the way, I'm a fan of collaboration. If you talk through things better with another real, live person, do it that way! Just make sure one or both of you are taking notes. This is the method I use with my clients. He or she talks and one or both of us write. The advantage to talking things through is that you hear what the words sound like. Remember, the written word and the spoken word are two very different things. The written word can be read at one's own speed, digested, reread for greater understanding. The spoken word is a one-shot deal. It must be in conversational language that is easily understood and digested as it is heard.

## Step 3: Create Your Threes

From these brainstormed ideas, see where commonalities lie. Can you group your main arguments into three categories? Are there three main problems that your audience is facing? If you've come up with eight problems, are a few the same thing, just said a different way? Your argument will always be stronger if you make these points distinct and clear. NOW is the time to look at what you've come up with and be tough with the red pencil. If you find you've identified only two real problems they're facing that your product or service or initiative will solve, keep at it.

Next look at the benefits (the GOOD STUFF) the audience will enjoy as a result of embracing your solution. Are there similar attributes to the benefits of adopting your idea or using your product or service? Group like things together. Be on the lookout for redundancies. Again, your results should be as distinct, clear, and compelling as were the problems. In fact, once you've clearly outlined the problem, your audience will be antsy for a real solution that offers solid let-me-sleep-at-night results. Make sure you get those down on paper.

## Step 4: Bullet-Proof It

Don't forget the Bespeak Persuasive Presentation format. You'll need to bullet-proof your claims of benefits. You've assessed your audience, so you have a good idea of what their objections might be. Write these down along with your rebuttals. NOW you've got a solid framework.

Nail It.

## Step 5: Determine Their Next Step

Figure out what your call to action will be. What next step do you want your audience to take? Figure this out now, understanding that as you rehearse it you may decide to alter it in some way. That's okay. This presentation isn't being written in stone. Yet.

## Step 6: Visuals

NOW is when you decide whether you want visual aids and what they might look like. If you know you have great charts and graphs that back up some of your main points, you may want to use them. If you're appealing to people's emotions on a BIG level (non-profits come to mind), you may want to gather some evocative photos. If the audience really won't benefit from seeing any kind of projected image, don't use PowerPoint. In fact, if you are speaking to a small group and you're presenting a product that's no bigger than a breadbox (or toaster, for those of you born after 1980), think about bringing the product as a visual. If your topic is mostly a motivational one, you may not need any kind of a visual. The audience's own minds may provide the very best visuals.

### Reminder

NO MATTER WHAT, you absolutely positively must not incorporate slides into your presentation simply because you need speaker notes. Visual aids are to aid the audience's understanding of the presentation. Speaker notes are for the (say it with me now) SPEAKER! DO NOT FORGET THIS. If you need to, reread the chapter on visual aids. If that doesn't work, contact me directly, and I'll give you a verbal thrashing over the phone, or worse, come to your home or office and deliver it up close and in person. Just save us both the trouble (and you, the agony), and DON'T DO IT.

## Step 7: First Walk-Through OUT LOUD — Working out the Kinks

Okay. Now you're going to put it all together and run through it. This will be torturous. Well, most of the time, and especially if you're doing it out loud and paying attention to what's coming out of your mouth. Sorry, it's unavoidable. The good news is, subsequent runs go much smoother. Here's the breakdown.

The first time through you're saying this stuff all together out loud. Let's say the beginning part goes smoothly. (Which often is not the case. I find beginnings change at least a few times in the course of developing a presentation.) Remember, you're not getting out the stone-carving tools at this point. At this stage we're still working with pencil and eraser and all the editing features available to you on our computer. Even assuming the intro sounds promising, as you get to your first transition, things begin to fall apart. You know you've got a killer first point, but getting to that first point from the intro is like crossing a huge canyon without so much as a good pair of Keds© (or for those of you born after 1980, Nikes©). You stop, hem, and haw, pace the floor. Not to worry. Simply give yourself a few minutes to come up with a good transition from your introduction to this first main point. You can do it. Heck, you came up with all the rest of the presentation. When you figure out what seem to be a good few sentences, write them down, start over at the beginning, and try them out. If they work, great, keep going. If not, go back to the drawing board. I hear you groaning. I know: it stinks. It's laborious, uneven, and just plain hard work. But if you can be patient and focused (and breathe, by the way), these bumps will smooth out, and you'll have a truly solid and beautifully flowing presentation.

Nail It.

> ## Nervous Speakers, This Is for You!
>
> PAY ATTENTION nervous speakers. It is exactly this kind of due diligence that will help your confidence level dramatically come show time. Why? Because you've worked out the kinks. You won't unhappily surprise yourself. You won't step in a hole you never saw coming. Your mind will not have to race around in panic trying to figure out how to connect point b with point c, because you already did that work in the privacy of your own home or office, not in front of a group of people watching and listening in real time. (Ah, you're getting sweaty just thinking about it, right? Well, take a deep breath and shake it off. This preparation will prevent that nightmare from happening to you ever again.)

Slowly and with focus, take yourself through the whole presentation OUT LOUD, stopping when you have to and coming up with transitions where you see they're needed.

You may also find you need to shift things around. Maybe your second point should come first. You hear yourself talking and realize you'll need to elaborate on something you'd planned to only touch on. You may find something that just doesn't fit. It doesn't belong in this presentation or is so big it needs a presentation all its own. It seemed like a fit when you were crafting the presentation, but now that you're running the whole thing, it's sounding out of place. Bravo! This is exactly what you want to happen. Just like the gaps where transitions are needed, discovering things that don't belong is something you want to know before you get in front of your audience.

## Step 8: PRACTICE, PRACTICE, PRACTICE

Practice. Yep, and more than once. I want you to practice at least THREE times once you've got the whole thing the way you want it. Stand up and practice OUT LOUD. Click through the slides if you're using slides. Hold up your product, if that's what you plan to do.

Nervous speakers, the absolute BEST thing you can do to diminish nerves is to practice out loud. Good speakers who want to be better, the same goes for you. The more our mouths get to practice saying the words, the more we hear ourselves say the words, the more confident we feel, the stronger our voices, the more convincing and compelling our messages. You must practice, and you must practice OUT LOUD.

If you're on a plane or train on the way to a presentation, you can take out a sheet of paper and (from memory) write down the main points, in order, of your presentation. This will write it on your mental hard drive, metaphorically speaking, and will build your confidence by helping you know your content. (It is not, however, a substitute for practicing OUT LOUD.)

The day of your presentation, practice the introduction and transition to your first point OUT LOUD. Why? Because it is at the beginning of your presentation that you will be most nervous. This is the part you need to be most comfortable with, and the only way to ensure that comfort is to practice OUT LOUD.

Nail It.

## Step 9: Check the Place Out

Assuming you'll not be speaking on your own turf, get to the site of your presentation at least thirty minutes early. If you're speaking at a conference, two hours before and even the night before is optimum. Stand where you'll be standing to speak. If there will be a microphone and it's there, try holding it and speaking. Don't feel bound by the physical layout. If your hosts have provided a podium, there is no reason you have to use it. Remember, podiums are barriers between you and the audience — never a good thing. If there's a stage but the audience can easily see you if you stand at floor level, allowing you to move among them, go for it. If there's a big piece of furniture (a table for panel speakers, for example), see whether it can be moved out of your way.

Being in the room the night before, or even a few hours before, will give you a much greater level of comfort. In fact, the room will become "yours." You will be welcoming your audience to YOUR turf. Which brings us to the next step.

## Step 10: Be the Host

Greet people as they come in. Not necessarily everyone, although at a conference where you are conducting a breakout session, I really like that idea. After all, attendees at a conference typically have about half a dozen choices of sessions, and they've chosen yours. Help them feel they've made the best one by welcoming them as they come in.

## Step 11: Take a Minute for Yourself

About five minutes before you are to speak, take a bio-break. Go to the restroom, check your teeth, your clothes, your hair. BREATHE. If you feel tense, do a few shoulder rolls. Shake out your arms and legs. If you've got a ton of nervous energy, jump up and down a few times. Look yourself in the mirror and smile. Say out loud, "This is gonna be great."

## Step 12: And, You're On!

As you're being introduced, pay attention to your introducer, and smile. Do not begin speaking until you are in front of the group (assuming this is a formal presentation). Even once you get in front of the group, give yourself a beat. Look at a few audience members, take a breath, smile, and begin. It is always easy to begin by thanking whoever invited and introduced you.

During your introduction or at some point during the beginning of the body of your presentation, let your audience know, if it's appropriate, if and when you'll be taking questions. Depending on the venue, you may also want to mention how long you'll be speaking. This kind of information puts audiences at ease. And with that ease comes the ability to focus on your message. Exactly what you want them to be doing.

## Step 13: Q and A

When you begin taking questions, remember to allow for even twenty seconds of silence before the first brave soul raises his or her hand. Remember to reward that person for asking the question. Let the audience know when you've got just a few minutes left and about how many questions you've got time for. This will allow them to self-select.

Nail It.

## Step 14: Last Words

Remind them of the call to action (schedule an appointment, fill out a form, turn in a business card, or whatever you want them to do next.) Thank them and smile. Then stick around, make yourself available to them and their questions and comments. Often you'll find audience members want you to listen to them. They will have a point of their own about something you said, and they want you to hear it. Some may disagree with something you've said. While it may be hard to listen with an open mind, I find the best response is something like, "That's an interesting idea. I'll give that some serious thought." Or, "What a great suggestion. Thanks so much for sharing it with me." If an audience member is getting emotional, raising his or her voice or using confrontational language, make sure you speak in a soft, even tone in your response. This will immediately make evident to the person his or her own behavior. Assure the person you've heard what he or she said, and that you hear the point. These two points are really the most important to anyone emotionally invested in an issue. You may have to disagree with them. If so, do it with a gentle tone of voice and evenhanded language.

Remember, these audience members felt strongly enough about you or your subject matter to seek you out after the presentation was over. You want to be gracious and appreciative no matter what their viewpoint.

## Step 15: Monday-Morning Quarterbacking

Depending on how your mind and memory work, you'll want to jot down a few notes about the presentation and how it went. I find that I am continually revising my presentations, albeit sometimes just a tiny bit, as I see what's working and what isn't. Every audience is different, but for heaven's sake, if three separate audiences are confused about the same concept, it's time to rethink the concept and your explanation of it. If your presentation keeps running long, it's time to get serious about editing it down. If you're not getting your desired result, it may be time to go back to the drawing board and start all over. Be honest with yourself. Evaluate and make changes where necessary.

### If it's not broke, don't fix it

Having said that, I would not recommend recreating the wheel every time you are to present. If you've followed the steps here as I've outlined them, you should have come up with a solid presentation. Sure, it may need tweaking. You may come up with new, better, more compelling examples or stories. But work with what you've got. Don't throw the whole thing out and start over. (That is, unless you didn't follow these steps and just cut and pasted a bunch of unconnected irrelevant stuff together the night before the presentation. THAT, you should absolutely throw out and start over.)

# 8
# Elevator Speeches

The elevator speech is your forty-five- to sixty-second "pitch" of you, your product, or service. It is called an elevator speech because the idea is that if you were to get into an elevator with your ideal client, you could describe what you do in the time it takes to go from the lobby to the thirteenth floor. A great elevator speech is constructed and delivered in such a way that the listener's response is, "Just what I've been looking for! Give me your card!" In other words, your elevator speech is a clear, concise, compelling statement of what you do.

These days, networking is an excellent way to market your business, and a great elevator speech is a must. Unfortunately, most people don't have one, or, more accurately, don't realize they don't have one. Thus, those of us in the small-business world are subjected to rambling, often confusing explanations that do nothing to convince us to use the speaker's product or service. Often, we aren't even clear about what it is the speaker does, let alone what the benefits would be of his or her product or service.

Nail It.

## Basic Characteristics

A good elevator speech requires a lot of thought and a lot of practice! It should be three things: simple, stirring, and short. Simple enough for an eight- or eighty-eight-year-old to understand and "get." Heads should be nodding. Second, it should be stirring. It should move people emotionally. Have you heard the saying, "People buy on emotion and justify with fact"? Boy, is that one true. In your elevator speech, you want to appeal to their hearts; their heads will follow. Think what they want (or don't want), not what they need. We all know broccoli and beets are good for us. But only those of us who like the taste (or want to eat healthfully) will eat them. We all know flossing is good for us, but only those of us who don't want gum disease (like, *really* don't want it) are flossing. Finally, you want your elevator speech to be short. No more than sixty seconds. If you've attended formal networking events you know that the person who goes well over his allotted time is the person no one wants to talk to after the meeting. Why? We're pretty sure that person will only want to talk more, and a lot. It's the person who gives the pithy pitch we want to bump elbows with. Shorter is always better.

## Part 1: Parts of the Pitch

What exactly goes into an elevator pitch? What are the essential components? So glad you asked.

### Who, what, and how (and possibly why)

These are the three (with a possible fourth) main components of a good elevator speech:

- **Who** you are and **who** your clients or customers are
- **What** your clients' or customers' problems are and **what** your product or service is
- **How** your product or service solves those problems
- **What** the results are

If you're in an overly saturated industry, you may want to provide the why: **why** you do what you do and **why** you're different from your competition.

## Who you are

"Hello, my name is . . ."

Your elevator speech should begin with your name and the name of your business. (Don't laugh. You'd be surprised how many people stand up, talk for a minute or two, and sit down without saying their name or the name of their company.) In fact, your elevator speech should end the same way: with your name and the name of your company.

## Who your customers are

Tell us who uses your product or service. Do you work with or sell to businesses or to consumers? If your target market is business, is it one type of industry? A certain department within any industry? Is there a size business you're targeting? A small business? Fortune 500's? (B to B or B to C?) If your target is consumers, what's your demographic: Women? Moms? Retirees? College grads? The more specific you can be the easier it will be for the listener to think "Hey, that's me!" or "That's not me, but I know someone who is." Either way, you're making yourself known. That's the whole point.

## What you do

Next, you want to tell the audience what you do. Stick to what matters to your clients, what they care about, what their problems are. Remember the 180° focus; keep sitting yourself in their seats. What brought your clients or customers to you? What was their pressing problem that you were able to solve?

If your business is about a product rather than a service, say what your product is. It's important that you use plain English. You'll be speaking to people from different industries and backgrounds, people I like to think of as "pedestrians." People you'd pass on a street or stand with in an elevator. Don't make the mistake of thinking you'll wow them with industry jargon and seven-syllable words. They can't think about hiring you or buying your product if they don't understand what you're talking about. Remember the eight- or eighty-eight-year-old rule. If those two age groups would understand your message, you're in good shape. If not, go back to the drawing board.

If your business is a service, talk about what you DO. Specifically, what you DO for your clients. Ideally, it should be something you do to solve a client's problem. The fact that you love doing it or that you've just begun doing it or that most people don't understand the ins and outs of doing it might be interesting to you, but I can pretty much guarantee, no one else is interested. Once you've figured that out — and it may involve different things for different clients — next think about HOW you solved their problem. Did you map out a game plan together? Did you simply begin? Did you suggest a plan of attack to your client that he or she then approved? What exactly did you DO? Explain it in one or two sentences in language the eight- or eighty-eight-year-old can understand.

## What your benefits (results) are

Next explain what your product or service does for these "who"s. What is the benefit (result) of using your product or service? Does it make their lives easier? Their businesses more profitable? More efficient? Does it give them peace of mind? Make them more beautiful? Healthier? Safer? Able to leap tall buildings in a single bound? Get the girl? Buy the sports car? You catch my drift.

## Why they should hire you

If you're in an industry that's pretty much saturated (fitness, graphic design, and financial advising are three that come to mind), explain how you're different. What makes you you better? Is it your background, your experience, your track record? If you can't easily differentiate yourself from others in your industry, tell them your philosophy, your perspective. Start with, "We believe . . ." or "Our approach . . ." This should be said in just a sentence. It may be difficult to do. You may find yourself stumped. Take the time to mull it over. Go for a walk and think about it. The time spent will be well worth it. That one sentence will inform the core mission and philosophy of your business. Being able to articulate those two things in a powerful sentence will garner quick identification, acceptance, and subsequent buy-in from your listener. If your business is self-explanatory (mine, for example), this isn't necessary. Ultimately though, it's great to know and be able to articulate succinctly and clearly how you're different from your competition.

Don't forget, every audience member is listening with the thought of "What's in it for me?" You have only about a minute. You want to give them the most compelling reasons to engage you or buy your product. You want to talk about what you do in an easy-to-understand-and-connect-with way. You want to pique their interest so they will want to learn more. You want to see heads nodding in comprehension and agreement. Stick to the information they want to hear: how you can help them or solve a particular problem they may have.

Nail It.

## Part 2: The Story — Problem-Solution-Result

The best way to illustrate what you do, for whom, and how it benefits them is by telling a story. Give them an example of someone who used your services or your product, what their need was, and how you filled it. This is the hook that helps them remember what you do, and it's the proof that what you do or sell really delivers. The formula for elevator-pitch stories is problem-solution-result. It looks something like this: We worked with a client who (Problem). Together we (Solution). As a result of our work together, they (Result). Stories are particularly helpful in a networking group that meets on a regular basis. If you will be involved in a group on a weekly or monthly basis, it's a good idea to "mix it up" a little bit. You don't want to recite the same speech over and over, week after week. How interested would you be in hearing your own elevator speech over and over, week after week?

The more stories you can tell and the more varied the examples, the more opportunities you give the listener for finding a way to either use you or refer you to someone who can. Be sure you include all three of these components. DO NOT tell the problem

### Yikes! I Hope That's Not Catching

When I first started my business I was a member of a weekly networking group. At each meeting we gave our elevator speeches. One of the members, an attorney, would often tell a horror story that had befallen a client of his. There was an audible gasp from the group as he described the legal hot water his client had found herself in. Then, having scared us all, he would smile and sit down. I didn't even want to sit next to the guy, let alone refer anyone to him. I knew he had clients with superscary problems. What I didn't know was how (or even whether) he solved those problems, or what happened to those clients once his work with and for them was done.

alone. DO NOT tell the problem and your solution but leave out the happy result. After all, we've all had the experience of buying a product that is advertised to help (weight loss comes immediately to mind) but doesn't. The clincher is the proof, and the proof is the result.

## Use real-life stories

How do you come up with different elevator speeches? Easy, you use your real-life examples. This is where storytelling is key. Tell success stories about client experiences and plug them into the problem-solution-result model. For instance:

"Hello, my name is Bob Thomas from Connect Computer. We recently got a call from an accounting office. Their mainframe had crashed. We went in and found that not only were they not running on enough memory, they weren't backing up. They were under tight budget constraints, having just merged with another accounting firm. We put together a package for them within their budget, and as of yesterday they're up and running with off-site backup. Again, I'm Bob Thomas, with Connect Computer."

Guess what? When that's your elevator speech, people are actually looking forward to hearing you week after week! Never forget that everyone loves a story, especially one with a happy ending.

## In casual settings, too

Stories are great in casual settings as well. Imagine I'm at a dinner party and someone asks me, "What do you do?" I respond with, "I'm a public speaking coach." "Really? What's that like?" "It's great. Just last month I worked with an exec who was terrified of public speaking and had to give a keynote at his annual conference. We created and rehearsed it together. He just texted me this morning to let me know it was a big success and he felt really good about it. Just doesn't get any better than that." (Now you can bet my dinner companion is thinking of people he knows who are terrified public speakers . . .)

Nail It.

Stories in elevator speeches are key. They give teeth to what you say you can do. By using a real example you not only give color and shape to your business, you let people know that you're out in the world doing it, and doing it successfully. Build your stories in the problem-solution-result format. Ideally, your audience should hear themselves or someone they know in the "problem"; this will make them listen eagerly for how you solved that problem and what the happy result was.

## The Rule of Threes and Elevator Pitches

The rule of threes works really well in elevator pitches. (Remember the rule of threes? The idea that human beings organize their thoughts in threes?) Here are several ways to incorporate the rule of threes into your pitch.

### Results

Ideally, you should have five great results or benefits (think all-star, spectacular, hit-it-out-of-the-park-type benefits) of your product or service. In an elevator speech you should name three of them. Remember, this is what your product or service does for your client or customer. It's not about the thingamajigs, hocus pocus, or doo-dads. It's about what result the client or customer gets from the thingamajigs, hocus pocus, or doo-dads. Make these three results as irresistible as possible. This is not the time to be modest, unassuming, or shy. Think Donald Trump (without the hair-do).

### Adjectives

This one's easy. Think of three adjectives that describe the benefits of your product or service. They should be BIG, BOLD, and BRAVE and should describe the good things (aka results) that will come from working with you or buying from you. Words like *fast, easy, reliable, dedicated, beautiful, immediate, long-lasting.*

## Alliterations

Alliterations are words that start with the same letter or sound. For example: *clear, compelling, concise.* These all begin with the *k* sound. *Simple, stirring,* and *short* is another example. Why is this a good thing? The human ear loves it. In fact, if you can think of three adjectives that begin with the same sound, you're hitting a double.

## Ideal clients or prospects

Are there three ideal types of industries you work with? Three ideal demographics for your product? In the "who" part of your elevator speech, you should list them. This gives your listeners a concrete idea of whom you do business with or who uses your product. You can list three companies you'd like to be introduced to. This is a great strategy if you're at a formal networking event. You'll be amazed. Inevitably someone there will have a connection for you.

## Services

Do you do seven things? Great, but please mention only three of them. If you're a member of a networking group that meets on a regular basis, you can rotate the three you talk about. A laundry list of your services is not going to increase your opportunities; it's going to overwhelm your audience. Speaking of which . . .

Your thought may be, "But I don't do only one thing" or "I don't sell only one thing." Fair enough. But in forty-five to sixty seconds, how much can you say, and how much can your audience remember? Not very much. This is especially true if you are in a networking environment. The listener may be hearing twenty or thirty elevator speeches in the course of a half hour. Stick to the magic rule of threes; tell them no more than three things you do or sell. Or better still, tell them one main thing you do or sell, with three parts to it.

Nail It.

If you were a painter, you could say you do residential and commercial, indoor and outdoor, basic and faux finishes. These are six "things," but we've paired them in a way that makes sense and is easy for an audience to understand and remember.

Someone who sells beauty products can say she sells make-up, skin care, and age-defiers. Again, three things, but all under the umbrella of "beauty and skin care."

### Warning! Don't Be the Chinese-Italian Restaurant

Often people will tell me that they do two completely different things and they want to talk about both of them in the sixty seconds they're allotted. This is what I call the mistake of trying to be the Chinese-Italian restaurant — a place I am never going to set foot in. Why? Well, other than the fact that they're both food, they have virtually nothing in common. When I drive by the Chinese-Italian restaurant I wonder which one of the cuisines they do well. I wonder, but I'm not going in to find out. Chances are good they don't do both well, and possibly they don't do either one well. I keep driving, looking for the restaurant focused on excelling at one cuisine. That restaurant will get my attention, my patronage, and my money.

If you've been an accountant for twenty-five years and now you're a realtor, pick ONE profession and talk it up. DO NOT talk about both. You may think you'll catch more fish with two nets, but I tell you, doing this will bring you up empty. Why? Think about it. If I'm hiring an accountant, I want to know come tax time that all his attention will be focused on my tax return. If I need a good realtor, I want to know she's working on selling my house, even in April! (In fact, especially in April, when the real estate market is smokin' hot). I don't want to worry that she's preoccupied with filing tax returns.

You're multi-talented, possibly multi–degreed and accredited. Bravo! Keep it to yourself. Pick one of the two things and spend your precious sixty seconds talking about it and only it.

## Part 3: Next Steps

You've stated whom you work with or provide a product to, what that product or service is, and how it benefits the recipient. You've told a story to illustrate, prove your claim, and create more interest. Now you simply close. "If you or someone you know (is in need of, is looking to, is having trouble with) ————, please contact me. (Your name, your company name.) We ————, (what you do or sell and its benefits)."

## Elevator Pitch DO's

### Practice

I know, you're thinking, "Heck, it's only a sixty-second thing. Not really even a speech. Why do I need to practice?" I'll tell you why: nerves. Remember Michael Motley's research? The stages of speech anxiety? These occur just before your presentation, increasing in discomfort until about thirty seconds into it. Well, thirty seconds in, you're half-way done. In other words, you're going to be having an out-of-body experience for about half of your elevator pitch. Yep, even those of us who love speaking and live for the spotlight have butterflies as we're giving our elevator pitch. The cure? Practice. You need to know your pitch by heart.

First, you want to practice it out loud so that you'll hear how it will sound to your audience. Once you're confident in the content, you need to practice so you know it will come out of your mouth even if you can't hear yourself talk over the pounding of your heart. Practice that morning in the shower and on the way to the event. Your heart rate will still be elevated, but your confidence will match it.

Nail It.

### Take your time

Wait for the person before you to finish. If he stood, wait until he sits, and wait until you are standing before you begin speaking. Even then, take a second or two and make eye contact with one or two people. SMILE, then say "good morning" (or another time-appropriate greeting) and begin. And don't sit down until you are finished talking.

### Look people in the eye

The whole idea of networking is connection. You connect with your eyes. If you look at someone and smile, they'll smile back. Score! Try looking and smiling at several someones.

### Smile

See above. Smiling makes your body feel good, makes those you're smiling at feel good, and causes them to smile back at you.

### Say thank you

If you are visiting a new group, it's always polite to thank them for having you.

## Elevator Pitch DON'T's

### Don't give out anything to read

As I pointed out earlier, people read and listen with the same side of their brains. Thus, if you give them something to read, a brochure for example, they will stop listening to you and start reading. If they're reading, you're missing out on your sixty-second opportunity to introduce yourself and your business. Most reading material gets thrown away anyway. Stick to your elevator pitch, and, at most, give out your business card.

### Don't read your elevator pitch

If there's one thing that screams "I really don't know what I'm doing" it's someone reading his or her elevator speech out loud at a networking event. If you don't know what you do well enough to talk about it for sixty seconds without a cheat sheet, stay home. You will only do yourself damage reading aloud about your own damn self. Seriously.

### Don't apologize

Do not begin by apologizing, telling the group how nervous you are, that you haven't really thought this through, or anything else that's irrelevant. Time is at a premium when you have only sixty seconds. Give your pitch and have a seat.

## What a Good Pitch Looks Like

"Good morning. I'm John Reilly with the John M. Glover Agency. We protect businesses like yours by finding and recommending the best coverage and the best price. Just last week I met with a couple. Both own their own business and work out of their house. We were able to get them better coverage on both their cars and their home and save them over $2,000 a year. By hiring us, you can focus your resources on obtaining more customers for your own business and not worry about insurance. If you or someone you know is wondering whether you're getting the best insurance at the best price, please contact me. Again, my name is John Reilly with the John Glover Agency."

John clearly states what he and his agency do for their clients, and thus, what they can do for you. He proves his claim by telling a story about someone he's recently helped. He lets us know he "gets" what's important to us: finding more business. Last, he states his name and his company at the beginning and end of his speech.

Nail It.

## Words Matter Here Too

Words are important. Dull, confusing words don't move us to action. Or if they do, they move us away from, not toward, the speaker. Use words that move people toward you, toward the service or product you are promoting. I like words like *compelling, change-making*, and *confident*. Words like *easy, trustworthy, reliable, understanding, rejuvenate, peace of mind, productive, partner, succeed, increase, uncover, discover, create, invent, reinvent, dynamic*, and *guarantee*.

These are words that evoke emotion in us. I confess that I am a fan of the "carrot" rather than the "stick." I prefer to appeal to peoples' hopes and aspirations rather than to their fears. I think when you speak positively, you get a positive result.

### More (and again) weak, wishy-washy words

The words below broadcast weakness, or at best, a lack of conviction. They serve only to undermine, diminish, and otherwise take the "oomph" out of your argument. Don't use them.

### *Maybe (might, perhaps)*

This is no time for being tentative. It's not "Maybe we can help" or "You might want to give us a call." Take a deep breath and say, "We can help." Or, "Give us a call." Be definitive. Be certain. If you say "maybe," I think, "maybe not." In a persuasive presentation you don't want to leave wiggle room.

### *Hopefully*

Of course there is a leap of faith involved in just about every undertaking, but you certainly don't want your audience to know that. "Hopefully you'll contact us" sounds as though you're living on a wing and a prayer, not on sound products and services. HOPE has nothing to do with the prospect, employer, or client contacting you, hiring you, or buying your stuff. It's the SOLID earthly benefits of you, your product, or your service. You must sound certain so that your audience will be certain about you.

### Sort of/kind of

You're not sort of an accountant. You're not kind of a nutritionist. If you can't talk about your product or service in absolute language, you may as well stay home. You can't expect potential clients to be very excited about your product or service if you are not fully committed to it.

### Consultant

I overheard one man at a networking event ask another what he did for a living. The second man answered, "I'm a consultant." To which the first man said, "No, really, what do you do?" Telling someone you're a consultant tells them nothing about what you DO. Narrow it down. Create a niche for yourself. It would be more effective to say you are a small-business consultant, a women's business consultant, a financial consultant. People need to know exactly what you do in order to use you, talk and think about you, and recommend you to others.

### Coach

See above. You must put an adjective (describing word) in front of this so that your audience has a crystal-clear idea of what you do and for whom.

Start paying attention to others in business, at networking events, even at cocktail parties. When you find yourself dozing off, confused, or clueless about what a person is saying, put a big red line through the words he or she is using and don't use them yourself.

Nail It.

## Tag Lines

A great tag line is something that should be repeated each and every time you give your elevator speech. That way people will be able to identify you and what you do easily and talk about you to others. My friend Steve Parmelee is a 401k benefit expert. His tag line is, "We help you get more, pay less, and get the paperwork off your desk." Another great tag line belongs to Victoria Koch, an attorney, "If you need an attorney, call me you must, Victoria J. Koch: honesty, integrity, and trust." It might seem corny, but people remember good tag lines — and the person connected to them.

## Take Aways

- Your elevator speech is your sixty-second pitch. It should be simple, stirring, and short.

- Your speech should say who you are and who your client or customer is, what you or your product does for them, and how it helps (what the benefits/results are).

- A story is always a great tool for proving your benefits and creating interest about you and your product or service.

- You must PRACTICE your pitch OUT LOUD.

- Do NOT read your elevator speech, ever.

- Do not hand out brochures or any other reading material during your elevator speech.

- Think of ways to use the rule of threes. Ideal clients, results, and adjectives are some of the applications.

- Watch your language! Use BIG, BOLD, BRAVE words, not weak, wishy-washy words.

- Mix it up: If you're attending a weekly networking meeting, be sure to tell different client success stories. This will make you someone others are eager to hear each week.

- DO NOT be the Chinese-Italian restaurant! If you are good at two completely different industries, pick ONE and talk about it and only it.

- If you have a great tag line, use it every time. It will help people remember you and what you do.

# 9
# The Job Interview: Your Most Important Presentation

You may not think of a job interview as a presentation, mostly because there are usually only two of you in the room. Nevertheless, the very same "Bespeakisms" that make for great presenters and presentations hold true for great interviews (and thus, great results).

## Be YOU

First, let's begin with the importance of being YOU. Quite often in an interview situation you want the job so badly you start thinking about "who they want you to be." It's a lot like clients of mine who want to "be a presenter like . . ." This is a bad news/REALLY good news scenario. The bad news is, you cannot be "like" anyone else. And if you could, how long do you think you could effectively keep it up? Wouldn't you exhaust yourself trying? Especially at a job, a place you're going to spend the better part of your weekly life, why in the world would you want to have to be anyone other than YOU? I know that a sense of very real urgency bordering on panic can set in when you think about job interviews. Remember, ideally you'd like to be in this new position for a while, hopefully about three years or more. It's important for you to make sure the company you are interviewing with will be a good fit for you. Take a deep breath and realize that you deserve to work in an environment where YOU feel comfortable. In fact, the more comfortable you are being yourself, the more energy you'll have to do the work you've been hired to do! That's a win-win.

## Turn Your Focus 180°

Second, don't forget to turn your focus 180°. You must put yourself in the interviewer's seat. What tasks will be required of the person who fills this position? What skills do you have that will ensure your success at performing those tasks? Think broadly about your experience. Think about volunteer work you may have done that could be applicable. Just because you weren't paid to do it doesn't make the work any less real or valuable. Write down these examples. Know them. You should be able to find ways throughout the interview to talk about these skills easily and readily. Which brings me to my next point.

## Practice OUT LOUD

As for any really good presenter, you must practice, and you must practice out loud. From the most basic question, "Tell me something about yourself" to the more complicated, "Tell me about a time you were conflicted about carrying out an initiative," you should anticipate all kinds of questions and have the answers easily within your mental reach. I am NOT talking about memorizing things word for word, unless you're a gifted actor (in which case I doubt you're reading this, or you shouldn't be — you should be reading *Variety* or standing in line waiting to audition!). Memorized answers will come off sounding stiff and disingenuous. Practice answering different questions, letting the answers come out as they will, and zoning in on key words and phrases.

## Solve Their Problem

Most important, don't forget that the interviewer has a problem he or she needs solved. The problem is that they have a slot open where a person should be, so important work either isn't getting done, or is getting done by someone with other important work he or she should be doing. YOU, the interviewee, are the answer to this problem. Your main objective in the interview is to let the person on the other side of the desk know that you have the skills, experience, and desire to be the solution to his or her problem.

Armed with the knowledge that you do, in fact, have more power than you might have thought, here are some other things to keep in mind.

### SMILE

Smile at everyone you meet beginning when your car turns into the parking lot. Make eye contact, with everyone. Thank the security folks in the parking lot and the lobby, the receptionist, the administrative assistant. Your goal is to WOW everyone in the place. Plus, smiling, making eye contact, and being gracious all broadcast confidence. As you meet your interviewer, look him or her right in the eye, SMILE, and offer a firm handshake.

### Handshakes

Speaking of handshakes, can we talk? Please, please, please, offer the interviewer a firm, but not crushing, handshake. DO NOT give them the dead fish (yuck) or the knuckle crusher (ouch). I've experienced both more times than I care to remember, and by members of BOTH sexes. A firm handshake that doesn't re-form the other person's fingers or joints is perfect. And important.

### Sitting pretty

When you are sitting facing the interviewer, your posture matters. Sit on the forward half of the seat. Your body should be leaning forward about 15°. This shows interest and connection with the person across the desk or table. Sitting all the way back in the chair makes it more likely that you'll slouch, lean to one side or another, or sabotage yourself in some other non-verbal way.

Hands folded in your lap is always a good way to start. As when presenting, do what comes naturally to you as far as gesturing goes. The interviewer is getting to know you. Sure, it's the on-your-best-behavior you, but the more you allow your natural speaking style to come through, the more he or she will see the person they'll be hiring. This will give them confidence in making a decision.

### No talking while they're reading

Although you undoubtedly will have sent your resume well ahead of the interview, most likely you'll bring one with you as well. I recommend waiting until the interviewer asks you for it to give it to him or her, but that's up to you.

What I am going to advise strongly is that you refrain from speaking while the interviewer is looking over your resume. Why? Because he or she can't read and listen at the same time. I know it may feel superduper uncomfortable to sit there quietly, but trust me and do it. When the interviewer looks up from reading, he or she will probably say something or ask you something, and then the conversation can begin. Anything you say while the other person is reading won't be heard, so you may as well just be silent.

## Tell 'Em a Story

The answers to many questions can have more weight if you tell a story to back up whatever statement you're making about yourself. Anyone can say they work well under pressure, but if you can tell a concise story about a time when you stayed cool while the world around you was crumbling, you give your claim teeth. More important, stories are easy to remember; they're sticky. You and your story will remain in the interviewer's mind long after you leave.

Think of the storytelling we talked about in the body of this book. Every story should have a beginning, middle, and end. So too should your answers to questions. Don't tell a story over and over, don't start in the middle and back track, don't give every minute detail. Again, practicing answers and the accompanying stories to likely questions will help tremendously.

## Listen Carefully and Answer the Question

Yes, you'll be nervous, but nervous or no, make sure you have your listening ears on. Be sure you hear the question and give the answer to that question. This may sound obvious, but I can tell you that having prepped my share of executives for high-level interviews, I've heard them go "around the world" (metaphorically speaking) and not get to the answer to the question. Again, this is why you must practice beforehand. You want to think through the most common questions and have concise, meaningful answers at the ready. Answer the question asked of you, and then stop talking. Don't bridge to another topic, UNLESS it's getting toward the end of the interview and you've not yet been asked a question you desperately want to be asked. (One whose answer would highlight a skill they're looking for or a challenge you dealt with successfully that is known to that position.)

### If you draw a blank

C'mon, it happens to the best of us. You're asked a question and seconds tick by while your brain is nowhere to be found. It's gone out for an ice cream, and you're sitting there like a ventriloquist's dummy. DON'T PANIC. Simply say something like, "That's an interesting question." And then repeat the question. That should give you just enough time for your brain to finish its little break and come to your rescue. If you've practiced the most common questions, this will only happen once or twice at the most in the course of the interview. Overall, you'll be articulate, calm, and collected.

Nail It.

## Stay Positive

NO MATTER what they say ("We're interviewing other candidates") or do (yawn, look at their watch, write things down), or even if your interview is interrupted by five phone calls and three people popping their heads in the door, stay positive and upbeat. SMILE again as the interview ends, give 'em that great handshake, thank them for the opportunity, and leave as you came in. Thank the receptionist, the security guard, and anyone else who greeted or helped you. You never know what the outcome will be. Letting ANYTHING get you down while you're there is a big mistake.

## Follow Up

I recommend sending a handwritten note and an email after the interview. The purpose of both is to thank them, possibly tell them something about you that may not have been said in the interview, and say something thoughtful and positive about the company and position. Each of these missives should be different, and both should be brief. Split up your comments and then send away.

---

## Take Aways

- Practice your answers to any and all questions you think you may be asked.

- Whenever possible, attach a story to your answer as proof of what you're saying.

- Be sure to listen carefully and answer the question that's being asked.

- Be sure your answers, including your stories, are clear and concise. Say it once and be done.

- Make sure you have a firm, confident handshake (but not a knuckle cruncher). Look everyone in the eye and . . .

- SMILE at everyone! From the moment you enter the property, you are "on." You want to make a great impression on each and every person you come in contact with.

- Do NOT talk while someone is reading. Wait until he or she finishes.

- If you forget the answer to a question, simply repeat it and say something like, "That's an interesting question" while your brain scrambles to find the answer.

- Thank the interviewer, and everyone else, on the way out. SMILE.

- Send a short email and a handwritten thank-you note, adding something about the company and your experience.

SO go forth and interview! Be YOU. Keep turning your focus 180°. Make sure you always keep your interviewers' needs in mind. (Never forget, it's about solving their problem, not yours.) And be sure to practice OUT LOUD, so you know you're giving a cogent and compelling answer to each of the questions you're asked. Do these things and you will be heard. And be hired!

# Conclusion: Start Today

We've covered a lot of important ground in this book. I want you to adopt this important, easy-to-follow information. Put it into action immediately.

Starting TODAY, trust that being YOU is more than enough and precisely the trick to becoming a compelling speaker. Audiences listen to people willing to offer themselves fully and truly. Gestures or no gestures, move around the stage or stay still — what matters most is being yourself.

Starting TODAY, build a presentation with the audience in mind. Turn your focus 180°. Sit yourself in their seats, think as they do, and then start building your presentation around them. Use words they can understand and connect with, phrases and themes and stories that will move, shake, and convince them.

Starting TODAY, commit to practicing absolutely everything you'll present. From interview questions to elevator speeches to pitches to boards of directors to sales presentations to keynotes. You must practice each and everything you'll be presenting, OUT LOUD.

Stick with these things, and the other practices and tools outlined in this book, and I promise you will be a confident, compelling, change-making presenter. The kind who gets heard and gets results. A speaker who nails it.

Start TODAY.

Go get 'em.

# Resources

To download your copy of the tools found in this book and on the following pages, go to www.bespeakpresentations.com, click on the **resource** tab (on the bottom right of the screen), and click on **Nail it.** In the pop-up login window, type **Nailit** as your user ID (note the capital *N*) and **nailitnow2014** as your password. You'll find the documents here that you can download and use for your own presentations.

## AUDIENCE ASSESSMENT TOOL

Determine as much as you can about your audience.
Answer the following questions:

WHO ARE THEY? (PEERS, SUBORDINATES, SUPERIORS, CUSTOMERS, PROSPECTS)

HOW MANY WILL THERE BE?

WHY ARE THEY COMING TO HEAR YOUR PRESENTATION? (EAGERLY, VOLUNTARILY, BY REQUIREMENT, UNDER PROTEST, WARILY, PESSIMISTICALLY)

DO THEY KNOW ONE ANOTHER?
ARE THEY AT ALL FAMILIAR WITH YOUR TOPIC?

Nail It.

**IF SO, DO THEY HAVE ANY PRECONCEIVED NOTIONS YOU MAY NEED TO DISPEL? LIST THEM HERE.**

**WHAT IS THEIR ATTENTION SPAN?**

**LEVEL OF INTEREST?**

## NAME FIVE REASONS YOUR TOPIC IS IMPORTANT TO THEM.

**1.**

**2.**

**3.**

**4.**

**5.**

> The more you know about your audience the easier it will be to create a presentation that appeals to them, addresses their needs, and gains their approval.
>
> Remember — all audience members are tuned in to the same frequency — WIIFM.

**be·speak**

## PERSUASIVE PRESENTATION FORMAT

POINT:


PICTURE: (AUDIENCE REALITY: PROBLEM/GOAL)


PROPOSAL: (YOUR SOLUTION)


PAYOFF: (WIIFM)


PROOF: (BULLET-PROOF YOUR PROPOSAL)


POSITIONING: (RECAP)


PROMPT: (CALL TO ACTION)

## ELIMINATE BABBLE-ING

| My Industry's Acronyms, Initialisms, Jargon Words | Definitions |
| --- | --- |
| | |

## LOGISTICS

Is this to be a formal presentation setting
or a more casual one?


Time of day? (Early morning, after lunch,
late afternoon)


Are you the only speaker?


If you are one of many, what number are you
in the "line up"?


Are they the ultimate decision makers, or will your
proposed idea require running it by someone else
before a decision can be made?

# References

Decker, Bert. *You've Got To Be Believed To Be Heard.* St. Martin's Press, 2008.

Mehrabian, Albert. *Silent Messages: Implicit Communication of Emotions and Attitudes.* 2$^d$ ed. Belmont, CA: Wadsworth, 1981.

Motley, Michael T. *Overcoming Your Fear of Public Speaking: A Proven Method.* Houghton Mifflin, 1997.

———. "Taking the Terror out of Talk." *Psychology Today* 22:1, 46–49 (Jan. 1988).

Oulton, Nicholas B. *Killer Presentations.* How To Books, 2005.

# Recommended Reading

DiResta, Diane. *Knockout Presentations: How To Deliver Your Message with Power, Punch, and Pizzazz.* Chandler House Press, 1998.

Toogood, Granville N. *The Articulate Executive: Learn To Look, Act, and Sound Like a Leader.* McGraw–Hill, 1995.

Waters, Lilly. *Secrets of Successful Speakers: How You Can Captivate, Motivate, and Persuade.* McGraw–Hill, 1993.